Arpeggios FOR BASS

by David Keif

The author wishes to thank Rodney Keif for
his invaluable contributions during the writing of this book.

ISBN 0-7935-7130-8

HAL•LEONARD®
CORPORATION

7777 W. BLUEMOUND RD. P.O. BOX 13819 MILWAUKEE, WI 53213

Visit Hal Leonard Online at
www.halleonard.com

Contents

INTRODUCTION

This book is written for bass players looking for a simple, practical method of learning and applying chord arpeggios. Adding these arpeggios to your practice routine will improve your technique and contribute to a complete understanding of the fretboard.

The chords covered are major and minor triads, major seventh, minor seventh, dominant seventh, and minor seven-flat five chords.

Scope

The exercises written for each chord are divided into two sections. Each section includes a brief introduction, a set of guidelines, and several examples of the arpeggio. These guidelines should be followed exactly, to maintain consistency among chord types (major, minor, etc.) and root names (C, C♯, D, D♯, etc.).

Practice Tips

The following tips will help organize your practicing and give you maximum benefit from this method.

1. Use a metronome or drum machine. Play all examples "in time" at a comfortable tempo. Work slowly through the material, but try to play each example using several root names at each practice session. Progressing through roots using the cycle of fifths (C—G–D–A...) is preferable to the chromatic cycle (C–C♯–D–D♯...).

2. Memorize each arpeggio spelling, shape, and location as quickly as possible.

3. Sing each example as you work through it, to teach yourself the sounds of these chords. This is very important.

These examples are written for the four-string bass. If you play a five- or six-string bass, extend the arpeggios through the range of your instrument.

PART ONE: TRIADS
1. MAJOR TRIADS

Let's begin with major triads. A major triad is a three note chord containing the root, a major third (two whole steps up from the root), and a perfect fifth (three and one-half steps up from the root). For example, on the root "C," the triad is spelled C–E–G. This spelling is called *root position.*

When we invert the triad by beginning with the second note, the spelling becomes E–G–C. This is called *first inversion.* When we invert it again by beginning with the third note, the spelling becomes G–C–E. This is called *second inversion.*

Figure 1-C Major Spellings

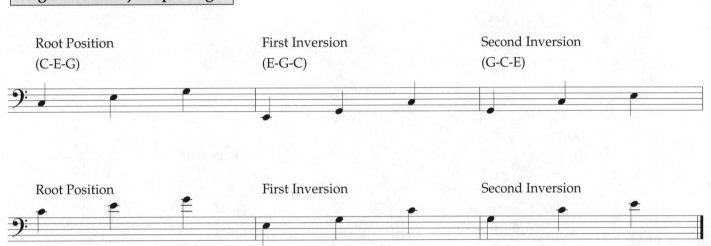

In order to arpeggiate (play through) any one of these spellings of the chord, a fingering pattern, or shape, is needed. It is these shapes which require our attention first.

While more than one shape exists for each spelling, it is important (for this method) to first find and consistently use only one shape for each. That means, for a major triad, there will be one shape for root position, and one shape for each inversion. Every time you arpeggiate a root position major triad, for example, it will have the same fingering shape regardless of where it is played on the neck. And that single shape will apply to all root position major triads regardless of the root name—"C" is the same as "G," "D," "A," and all of the others.

This also applies to the two inversions of the triad. There is one shape for first inversion and another for second inversion, regardless of location on the neck or name of the root.

All notes should be fretted; do not include open strings in a shape.

It is important to quickly recognize and identify triads in first and second inversions; they are just as important and useful as those in root position.

When working through the exercises, note that all triads begin with the lowest possible version on the neck, even if it is not the root position of that triad. In other words, some arpeggios may begin with the first or second inversion in order to cover that triad's full range on the neck.

The last guideline to keep in mind is that each shape will be played without a shift of the hand. Shifting may occur between shapes, but each shape will be played in one hand position.

Guidelines for Major Triads

Three spellings	Notes
Root position	(1-3-5)
First inversion	(3-5-1)
Second inversion	(5-3-1)

One fingering shape per spelling, consistent among all root names and locations on the neck.

	Fingering
Root position	2-1-4
First inversion	1-4-4
Second inversion	2-2-1

No open strings included in fingering shape.

Arpeggiations begin with the lowest possible spelling on the fretboard.

No position shifts during the arpeggiation of a spelling—only between spellings.

C MAJOR (C)

Starting with C major, use the three fingering shapes in Figure 2 to play the arpeggio. Because G is the lowerst note that can be played in this triad—remember, no open strings—we will begin with the second inversion (G–C–E) and play each of the three spellings in one position (are of the neck) without pausing. The resulting arpeggios should sound smooth and connected. It is very important to recognize and memorize the note names in addition to the shapes.

Begin this arpeggio with second inversion (G on the E string). This should be played in one position (area of the neck). Numbers below the fretboard diagrams indicate fret numbers.

Figure 2

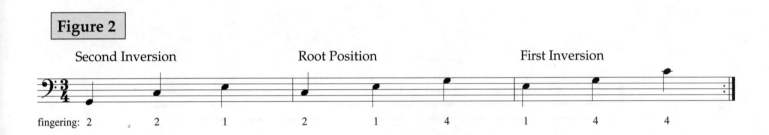

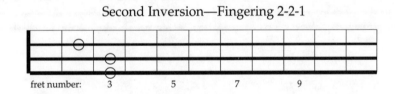

Second Inversion—Fingering 2-2-1

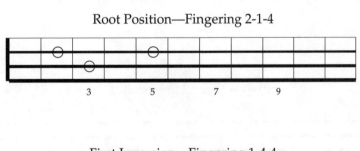

Root Position—Fingering 2-1-4

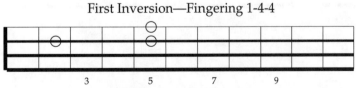

First Inversion—Fingering 1-4-4

7

Moving up to the eighth fret (C on the E string), repeat the arpeggio shapes, this time beginning with root position. In order to maintain the proper fingering, a two fret shift of the hand is required between the first and second inversions. The shift occurs between first finger (the note E on the A string) and second finger (the note G on the on the A string), and should take place after the completion of the arpeggio for first inversion.

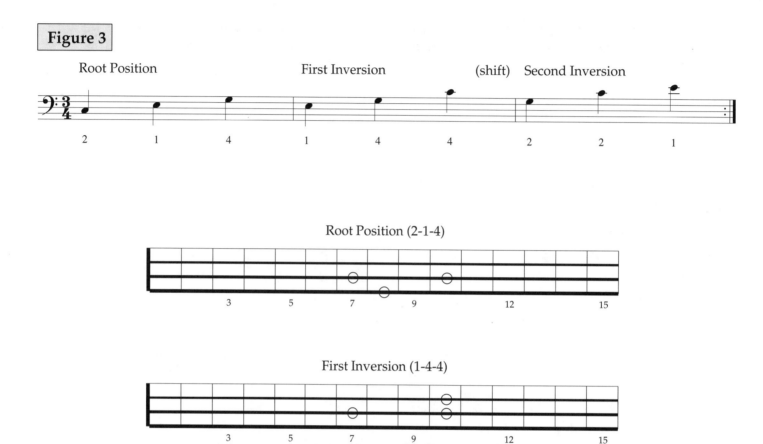

In order to maintain a consistent shape for second inversion (2-2-1), a two fret shift is necessary between first inversion and second inversion.

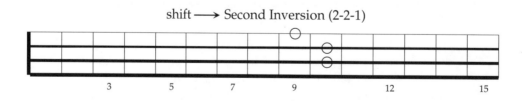

To cover the last area of the neck for the C major triad, move to the twelfth fret (E on the E string) and begin the arpeggio, this time starting with the first inversion. Like the last position, a hand shift is required between first and second inversions. In this area of the neck, a repeat of the first inversion is also available one octave higher and it should be included in the arpeggio. Play this sequence repeatedly.

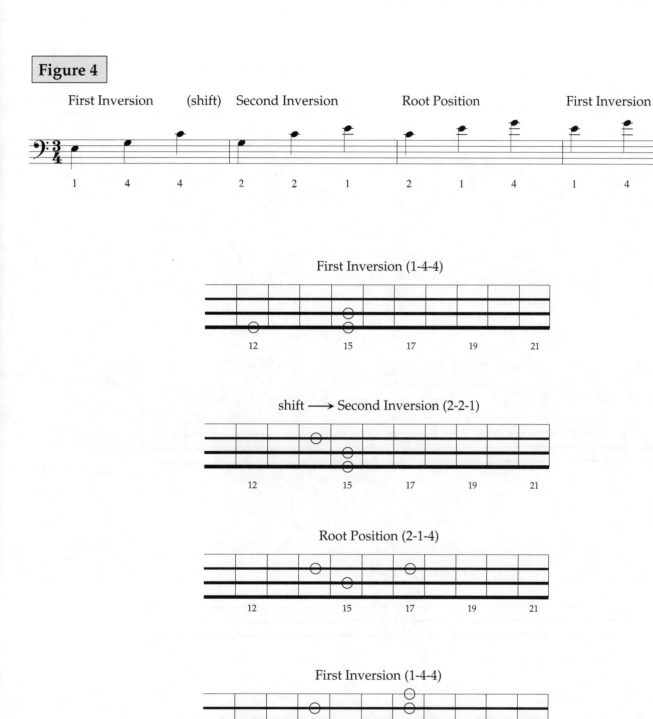

Before moving to the next section, review the three areas of the neck we just covered. Remember that when played properly, only three fingering shapes are used—one for each spelling. Play each position until the chord spellings and shapes are memorized.

In this section, we will begin each triad on the same string. Arpeggios will not be played in a single area of the neck—each version will begin in a new position. Using C major as the example, begin the arpeggio in second inversion (third fret G on the E string), follow it with root position (eighth fret on the E string), and finish with first inversion (twelfth fret on the E string). The shifts should be quick and smooth, so that the arpeggio sounds as if it was played in one position.

Figure 5 shows each version of the C major triad beginning on the E string.

Figure 5

Second Inversion   Root Position   First Inversion

Second Inversion (2-2-1)

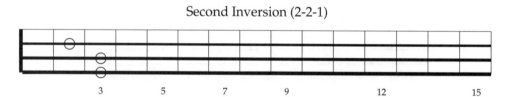

Root Position (2-1-4)

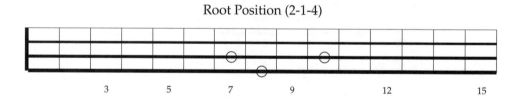

First Inversion (1-4-4)

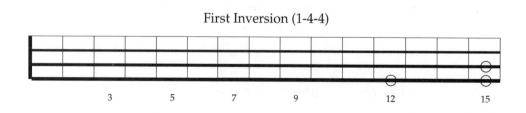

Next, apply this approach on the A string. Start the arpeggio in root position (C at the third fret of the A string), followed by the first inversion at the seventh fret, and second inversion at the tenth fret. Again shifts occur between versions, but the shapes remain consistent with the previous examples. Play repeatedly until this sequence is memorized.

Figure 6 shows each version of the C major triad beginning on the A string.

Figure 6

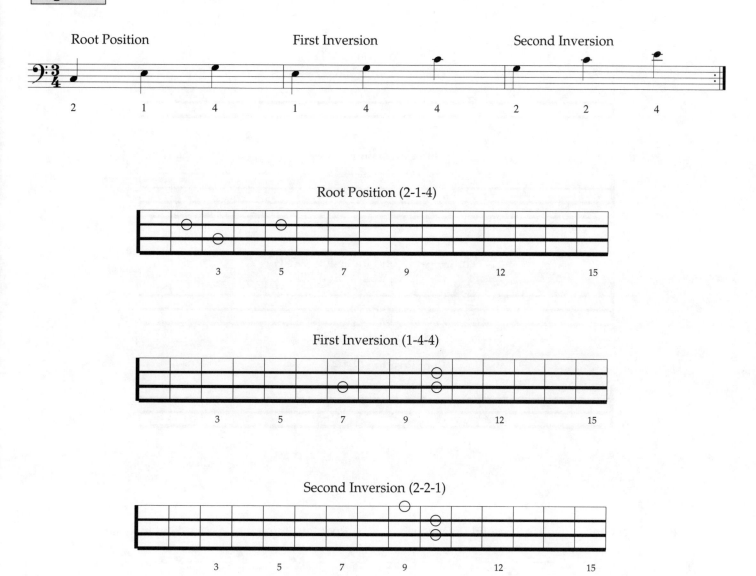

After a review of the C major triad, apply this system of study to different chord names (G, D, A, etc.): First, practice all versions in one area at a time, then practice each version beginning on the same string in a different position on the neck. All names should be covered; however, it is best to work slowly and methodically. Each chord name will have exactly the same three shapes, but will begin in a different place.

For instance, the C arpeggio begins with the second inversion as the lowest possible spelling, but the G triad begins with root position. Always play the full range of the arpeggio. Arpeggios for G and D are included here to get you started.

G MAJOR (G)

Play the next three figures each in one area of the neck.

Figure 7

Root Position   First Inversion   (shift) Second Inversion   Root Position

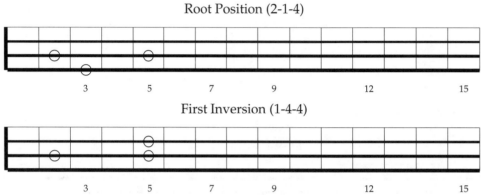

Root Position (2-1-4)

First Inversion (1-4-4)

shift ⟶ Second Inversion (2-2-1)

Root Position (2-1-4)

Figure 8

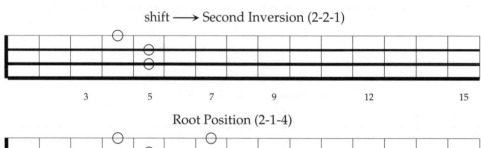

First Inversion   (shift) Second Inversion   Root Position   First Inversion

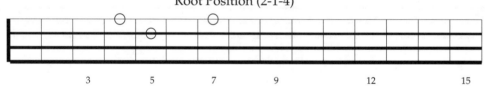

First Inversion (1-4-4)

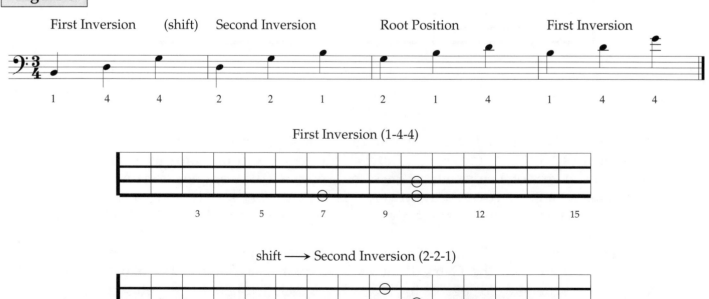

shift ⟶ Second Inversion (2-2-1)

Root Position (2-1-4)

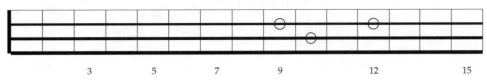

First Inversion (1-4-4)

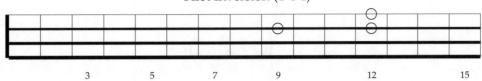

Figure 9

Root Position (2-1-4)

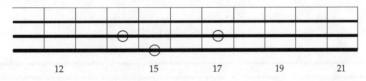

First Inversion (1-4-4)

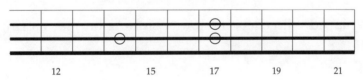

shift ⟶ Second Inversion (2-2-1)

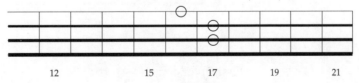

Root Position (2-1-4)

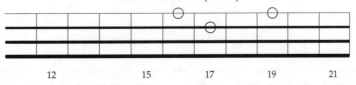

Figure 10 is played with each version beginning on the E string.

Figure 10

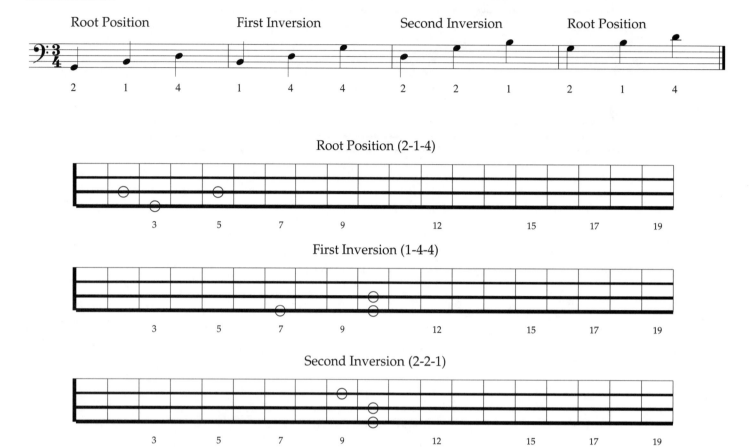

Root Position (2-1-4)

First Inversion (1-4-4)

Second Inversion (2-2-1)

Root Position (2-1-4)

Figure 11 is played with each version beginning on the A string.

Figure 11

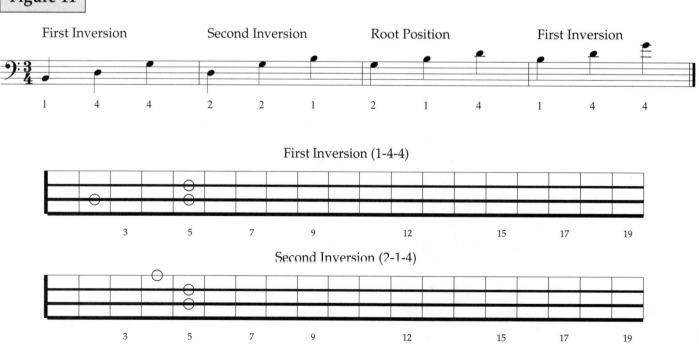

First Inversion (1-4-4)

Second Inversion (2-1-4)

Root Position (2-1-4)

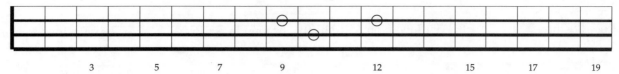

First Inversion (1-4-4)

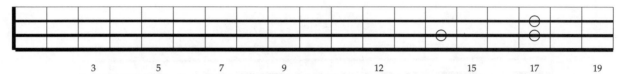

D MAJOR (D)

Figure 12

First Inversion   (shift)   Second Inversion   Root Position   First Inversion

First Inversion (1-4-4)

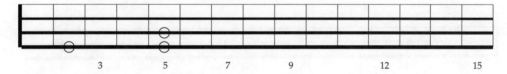

shift ⟶ Second Inversion (2-2-1)

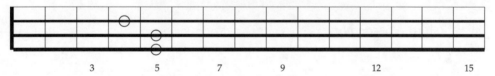

Root Position (2-1-4)

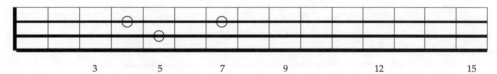

First Inversion (1-4-4)

Figure 13

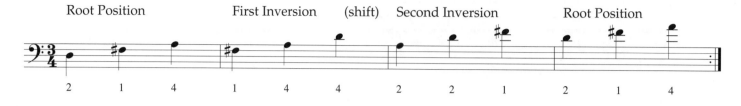

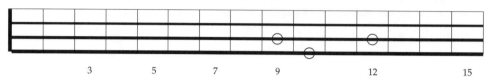

Root Position (2-1-4)

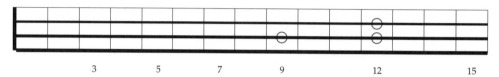

First Inversion (1-4-4)

shift ⟶ Second Inversion (2-2-1)

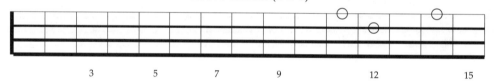

Root Position (2-1-4)

Figure 14

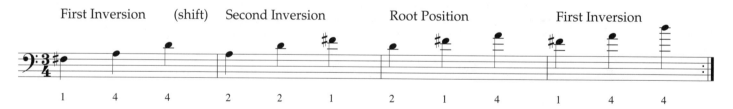

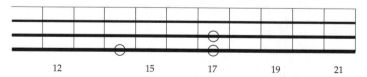

First Inversion (1-4-4)

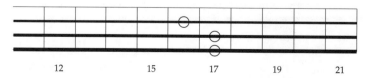

shift ⟶ Second Inversion (2-2-1)

Root Position (2-1-4)

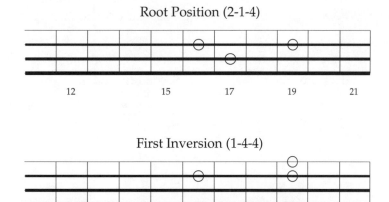

First Inversion (1-4-4)

Figure 15 is played with each version beginning on the E string.

Figure 15

First Inversion   Second Inversion   Root Position   First Inversion

First Inversion (1-4-4)

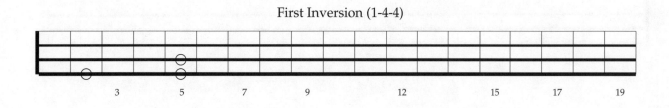

Second Inversion (2-2-1)

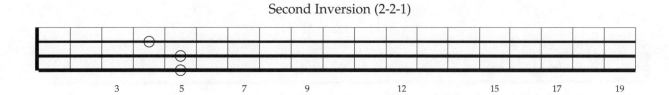

Root Position (2-1-4)

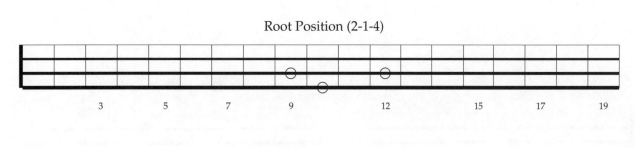

First Inversion (1-4-4)

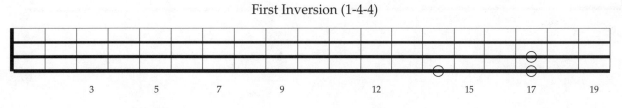

Figure 16 is played with each version beginning on the A string.

Figure 16

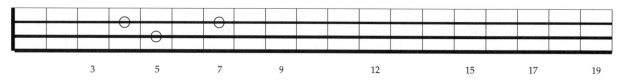

Root Position (2-1-4)

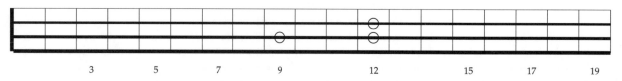

First Inversion (1-4-4)

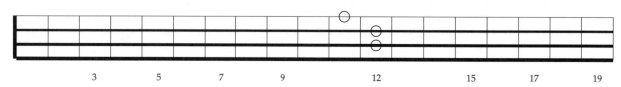

Second Inversion (2-2-1)

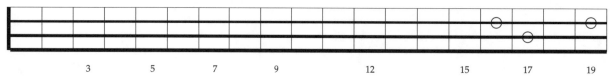

Root Position (2-1-4)

2. MINOR TRIADS

Minor triads will be studied exactly as the major triads were. A minor triad contains the root, a minor third (two and one-half steps above the root), and a perfect fifth (three and one-half steps above the root). Each version of a minor triad will have one shape which is consistent in all positions and among all root names.

Play all three versions of each chord. Beginning at the lowest place on the neck (remember, no open strings in the fingering shapes), play all the possible versions in one position before moving to the next. After all the positions have been covered, play each version starting from the E string only (which will require a position shift between versions) and then the A string (also a shift between versions).

Again, the figures given are for roots C, G, and D, but the information applies to all the root names. It is very important to apply this method to all of the minor triads. Play each arpeggio repeatedly in order to memorize the sound, shape, and the proper triad spelling. Compare the sounds and shapes of the minor triads with those of the major triads.

Guidelines for Minor Triads

Three spellings	Notes
Root position	(1-♭3-5)
First inversion	(♭3-5-1)
Second inversion	(5-1-♭3)

One fingering shape for each spelling, consistent among all root names and locations on the neck.

	Fingering
Root position	1-4-3
First inversion	2-1-1
Second inversion	1-1-4

No open strings included in fingering shape.

Arpeggiations begin with the lowest possible spelling on the fretboard.

No position shifts during the arpeggiation of a spelling—only between spellings.

C MINOR (Cm)

To begin the C minor triad, start with the second inversion (G–C–E♭) at the third fret on the E string. Follow that with root position (C–E♭–G) at the third fret on the A string, then make a two-fret shift (first finger C to second finger E♭) to set up the correct fingering for the first inversion (E♭–G–C) starting at the sixth fret. Complete the arpeggio with a repeat of the second inversion at the fifth fret on the D string. Play repeatedly until the arpeggio is smooth and connected.

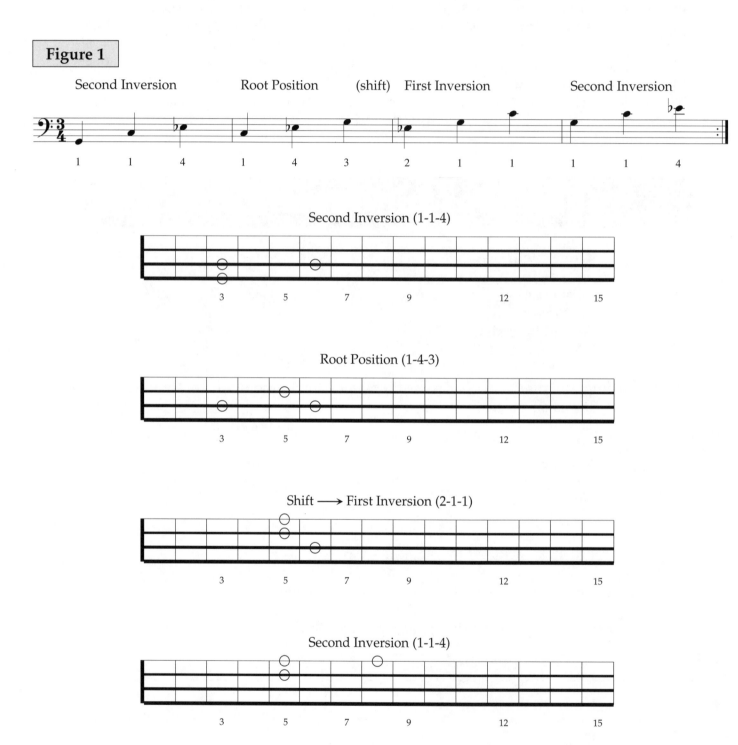

20

Continue the arpeggio now at the eighth fret, beginning with root position. Follow that with a two-fret shift to first inversion (E♭ on the E string), and then second inversion (G on the A string). Finish this area in root position (C on the D string).

Figure 2

Root Position   (shift) First Inversion   Second Inversion   Root Position

Root Position (1-4-3)

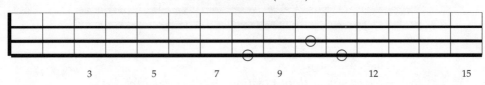

shift ⟶ First Inversion (2-1-1)

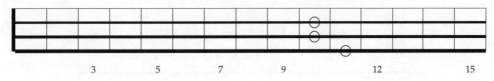

Second Inversion (1-1-4)

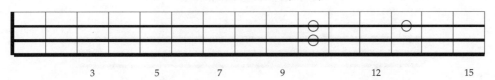

Root Position (1-4-3)

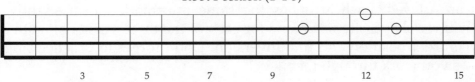

The last area of study for C minor begins at G (fifteenth fret) on the E string. Start this position with the second inversion. Next is root position (C on the A string), first inversion (don't forget the shift), and then the repeat of second inversion. Play this figure and figures in every area of the neck until the arpeggio is memorized.

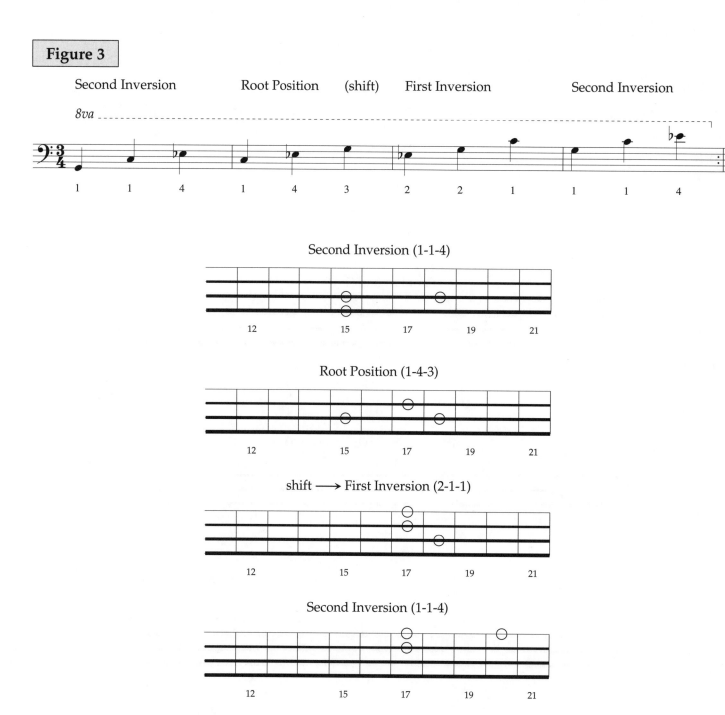

Figure 3

Before moving on to the next section, review all three areas where C minor arpeggios are played. Each area has the same information in a slightly different order. Only three shapes are used (one for each of the three versions), with a two-fret shift between root position and first inversion. Don't forget to practice singing these arpeggios as you work through them!

In this section, each spelling of the triad will be played beginning on the same string. Arpeggios will not be played in a single area of the neck, but rather each version will begin in a new position. Using C minor as the example, begin the arpeggio on the third fret with the second inversion (G on the E string) and follow it directly with root position at the eighth fret on the E string, and then the first inversion at the eleventh fret on the E string. Finish with a repeat of second inversion at the fifteenth fret. The shifts should be quick and smooth, so that the arpeggio sounds as if it were played in one position.

Figure 4 shows each version of the C minor triad beginning on the E string.

Figure 4

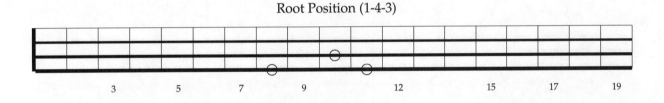

Second Inversion (1-1-4)

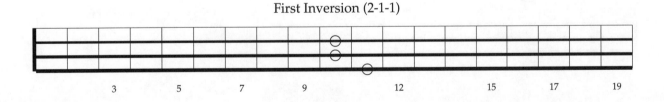

Root Position (1-4-3)

First Inversion (2-1-1)

Second Inversion (1-1-4)

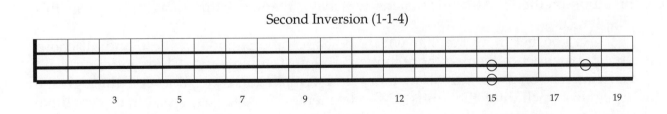

Next, play each version starting on the A string. This will require a shift to a new position between versions of the arpeggio. Begin with root position (third fret C on the A string), and continue up the neck with first inversion, second inversion, and finish with root position.

Figure 5 shows each version of the C minor triad beginning on the A string.

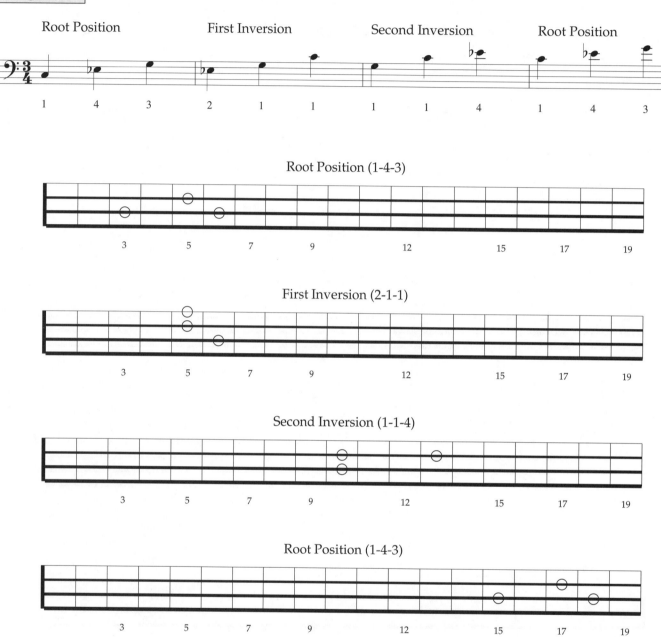

After a review of C minor, continue the study of minor triads using the previous methods. All minor triads will have the same three shapes used in this chapter.

As you get more familiar with the shapes and sounds of these and all chord arpeggios, practice them without looking at your fretting hand. Close your eyes and learn to rely on your muscle memory and visualization to guide you through the arpeggios (including the shifts). Muscle memory occurs as a result of repetitive action (i.e., practicing these arpeggios) and visualization is the ability to picture in your mind the action which you plan to take. Both skills will come as you spend the necessary time to master these exercises.

Now learn and practice minor triads on all the root names. Arpeggios built on G and D are included here to get you started.

G MINOR (Gm)

Play the next three figures each in one area of the neck.

Figure 6

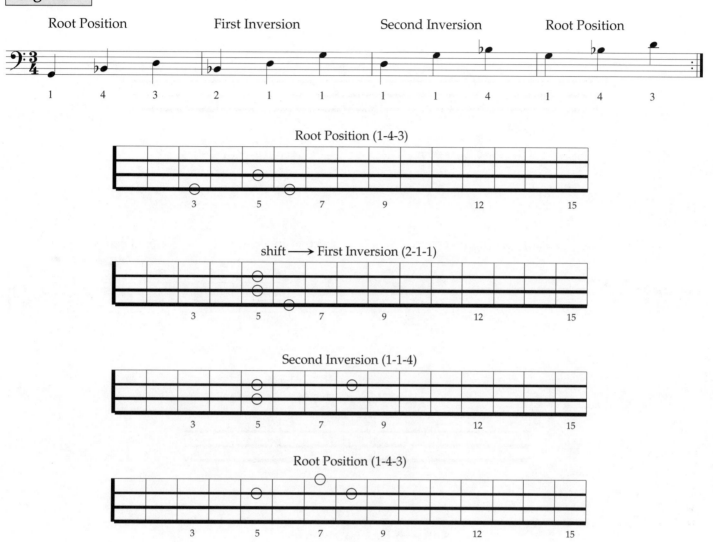

Figure 7

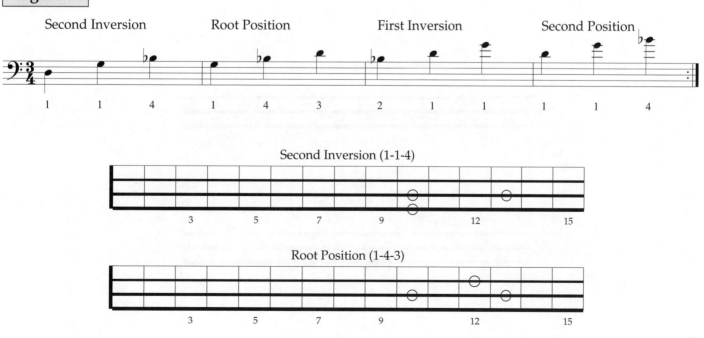

shift ⟶ First Inversion (2-1-1)

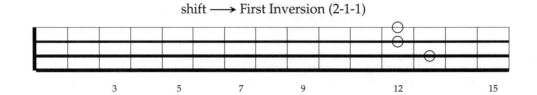

Second Inversion (1-1-4)

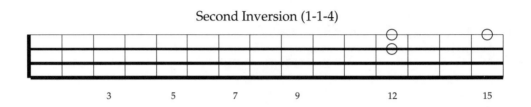

Figure 8

Root Position   (shift)   First Inversion   Second Inversion   Root Position

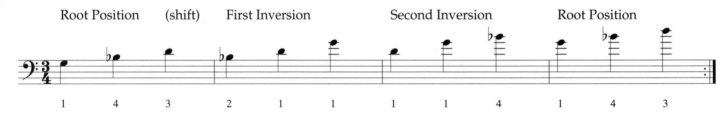

Root Position (1-4-3)

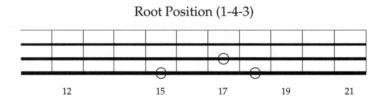

shift ⟶ First Inversion (2-1-1)

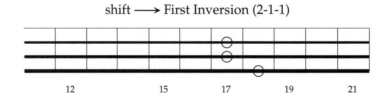

Second Inversion (1-1-4)

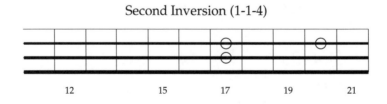

Root Position (1-4-3)

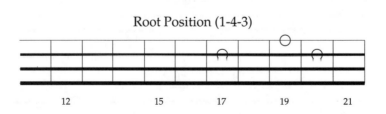

Now play each version beginning on the E string.

Figure 9

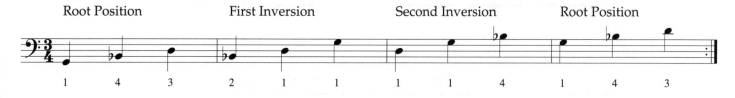

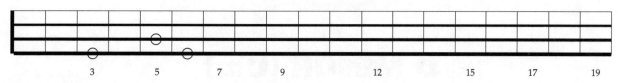

Root Position (1-4-3)

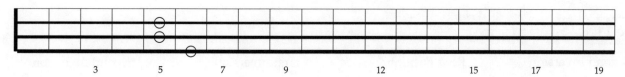

First Inversion (2-1-1)

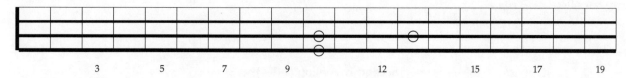

Second Inversion (1-1-4)

Root Position (1-4-3)

Now play each version beginning on the A string.

Figure 10

Second Inversion (1-1-4)

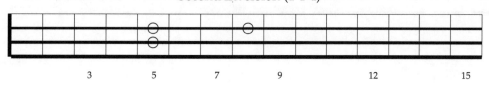

Root Position (1-4-3)

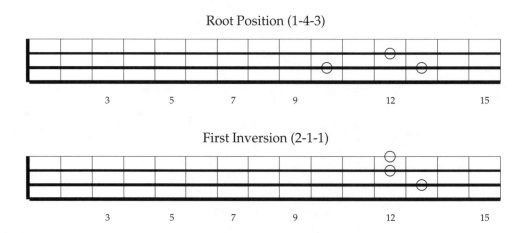

First Inversion (2-1-1)

D MINOR (Dm)

Play the next three figures each in one area of the neck.

Figure 11

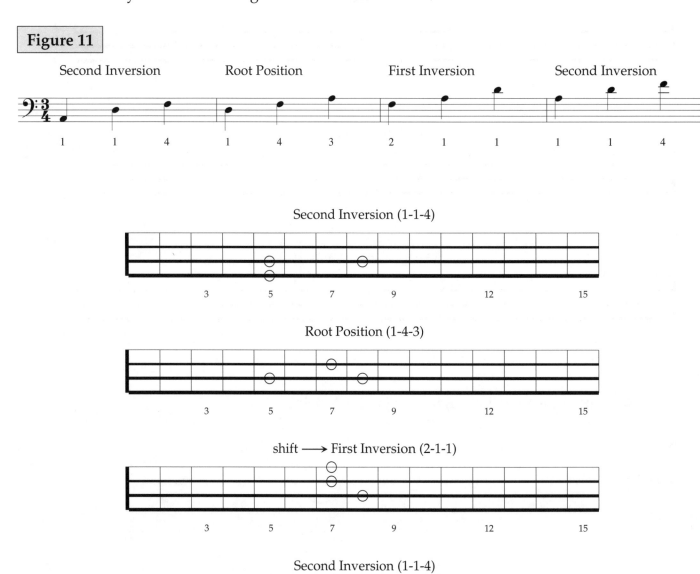

Second Inversion (1-1-4)

Root Position (1-4-3)

shift ⟶ First Inversion (2-1-1)

Second Inversion (1-1-4)

Figure 12

Root Position   (shift)   First Inversion   Second Inversion   Root Position

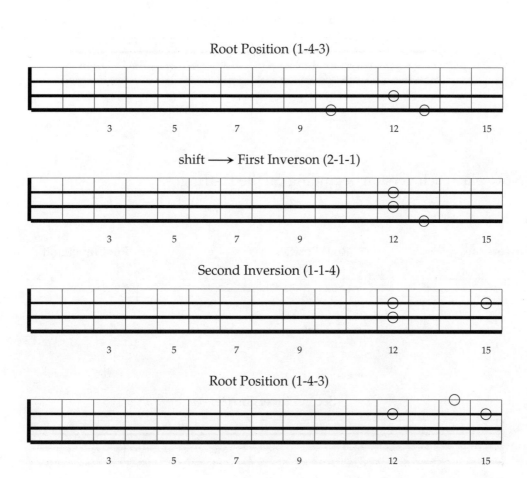

Root Position (1-4-3)

shift ⟶ First Inverson (2-1-1)

Second Inversion (1-1-4)

Root Position (1-4-3)

Figure 13

Second Inversion   Root Position   (shift)   First Inversion   Second Inversion

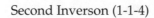

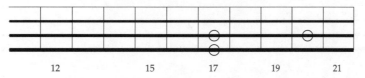

Second Inverson (1-1-4)

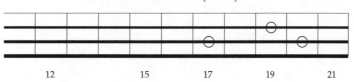

Root Position (1-4-3)

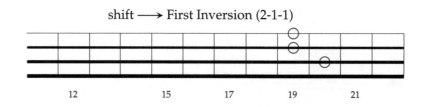

Second Inversion (1-1-4)

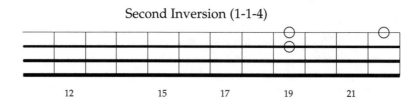

Now play each version beginning on the E string.

Figure 14

Second Inversion   Root Position   First Inversion

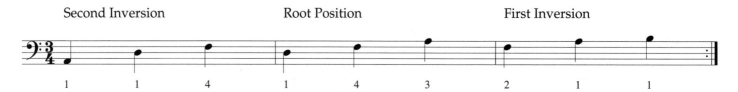

Second Inversion (1-1-4)

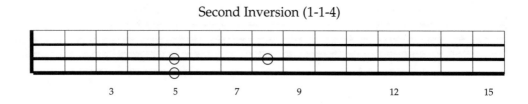

Root Position (1-4-3)

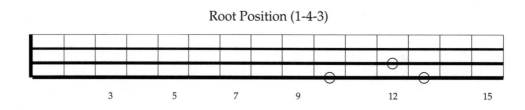

First Inversion (2-1-1)

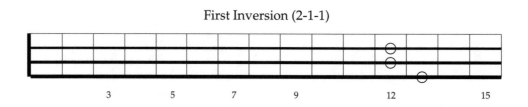

Now play each version beginning on the A string.

Figure 15

Root Position   First Inversion   Second Inversion

1   4   3   2   1   1   1   1   4

Root Position (1-4-3)

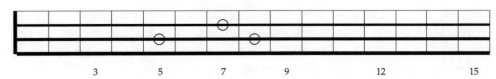

First Inversion (2-1-1)

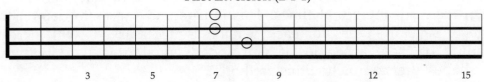

Second Inversion (1-1-4)

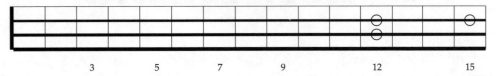

PART TWO: SEVENTH CHORDS

This is the second half of a book for the player seeking a systematic, practical approach for learning and applying chord arpeggios on the electric bass. The information is a continuation of the first half, which covered triads. You should be familiar with the triad study before proceeding with seventh chords. This book will contribute to an improved understanding of major diatonic harmony and its applications on the fretboard.

When the major scale is harmonized (chords built on each scale degree), it produces four types of seventh chords: major seventh, minor seventh, dominant seventh, and minor seventh-flat five. The arpeggiation of these chords is the focus of this part of the book.

The arpeggio exercises adhere to a specific set of guidelines which should be precisely followed. These guidelines are designed to maintain a consistency among each chord type and root name. Following this system will lead to an improved understanding of these chords and the creative use of them.

Practice these arpeggios with a metronome or a drum machine. Play through each example using several root names per practice session, and progress through those roots by the cycle of fifths (C–G–D–A–E–B–F♯–C♯) rather than chromatically.

The examples are written for four-string bass. If you are playing a five- or six-string, it is important to include the extended range of your instrument during the practice of these arpeggios.

As you work through these seventh chords, it may seem that alternate shapes to those given have advantages at times. This is true and serves to demonstrate that knowledge of several shapes for each version is necessary. It will increase your understanding of these arpeggios if you spend equal time working with these alternates shapes after completing this method.

Finally, it is particularly important to remember that although this method is the study of chord shapes, it is essential to memorize the chord spellings and sounds to gain complete command of chord arpeggios. Play each example repeatedly, and practice singing the exercises as you play them.

5. MAJOR SEVENTH

A seventh chord is a triad with another note added. This note is the interval of either a major, minor, or diminished seventh above the root of the chord. A major seventh chord (maj7) is a major triad with a major seventh added. Built on the root C, the major seventh is spelled C–E–G–B. This is the spelling for root position. First inversion is spelled E–G–B–C. Second inversion is spelled G–B–C–E. Because of the addition of a fourth note (the seventh) to the chord, there is a third inversion as well, which is spelled B–C–E–G. In order to arpeggiate through this chord type, a fingering pattern (shape) for each spelling is necessary.

Although more than one shape for each version is available, the most effective learning system is to use only one shape per spelling. This means for every major seventh chord, regardless of the root name or location on the neck, there are only four fingering shapes (one for each version). In other words, each time you arpeggiate a root position major seventh chord, it will have a fingering pattern that applies to all root names and locations on the neck. The same applies for first, second, and third inversions.

As with triads, no shifting will occur during a finger shape. All shifting for arpeggios will happen between versions. Also remember that no open strings will be a part of a shape; all notes should be fretted. In order to take advantage of the full range of the instrument, all arpeggios will begin at the lowest possible, even if it is not the root position of the chord. Many chords will begin with an inversion.

Each chord will be arpeggiated first in one general area played across the neck and then beginning from one string only and played up the neck.

Guidelines for Major Seventh Chords

Four spellings	Notes
Root position	(1-3-5-7)
First inversion	(3-5-7-1)
Second inversion	(5-7-1-3)
Third inversion	(7-1-3-5)

One fingering shape per spelling, consistent among all root names and locations on the neck.

	Fingering
Root position	2-1-4-3
First inversion	1-4-3-4
Second inversion	2-1-2-1
Third inversion	1-2-1-4

No open strings included in fingering shape.

Arpeggiations begin with the lowest possible spelling on the fretboard.

No position shifts during the arpeggiation of a spelling—only between spellings.

C MAJOR SEVENTH (Cmaj7)

Using C as the root, arpeggiate a major seventh chord starting with the second inversion (third fret G on the E string). Play all four versions in this position. Note that no position shift is required in this area of the neck. Play this arpeggio repeatedly in order to memorize the spellings and shapes.

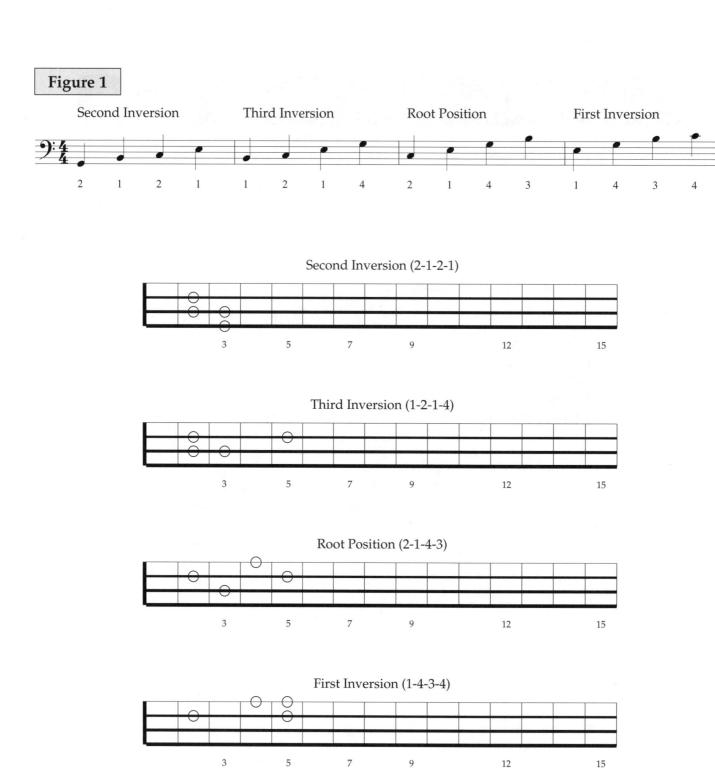

The next area for C major seventh begins with the third inversion (B on the E string) at the seventh fret. Follow this with root position and then first inversion. A two-fret shift of the hand (first finger E to second finger G) is necessary between first and second inversions to maintain the proper fingering. This will allow for the arpeggio to continue with a repeat of third inversion.

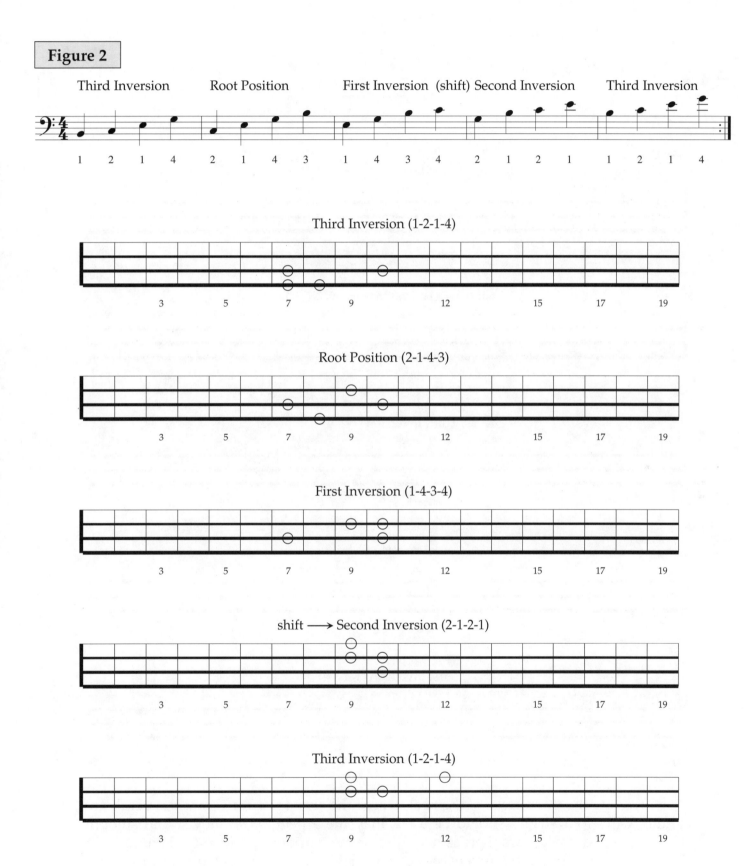

Figure 2

Third Inversion   Root Position   First Inversion (shift) Second Inversion   Third Inversion

1   2   1   4   2   1   4   3   1   4   3   4   2   1   2   1   1   2   1   4

Third Inversion (1-2-1-4)

3   5   7   9   12   15   17   19

Root Position (2-1-4-3)

3   5   7   9   12   15   17   19

First Inversion (1-4-3-4)

3   5   7   9   12   15   17   19

shift ⟶ Second Inversion (2-1-2-1)

3   5   7   9   12   15   17   19

Third Inversion (1-2-1-4)

3   5   7   9   12   15   17   19

The last area begins at the twelfth fret, where a first inversion occurs. An immediate two-fret shift is necessary, followed by second inversion, third inversion, root position and a repeat of first inversion. Play repeatedly until the arpeggio is memorized.

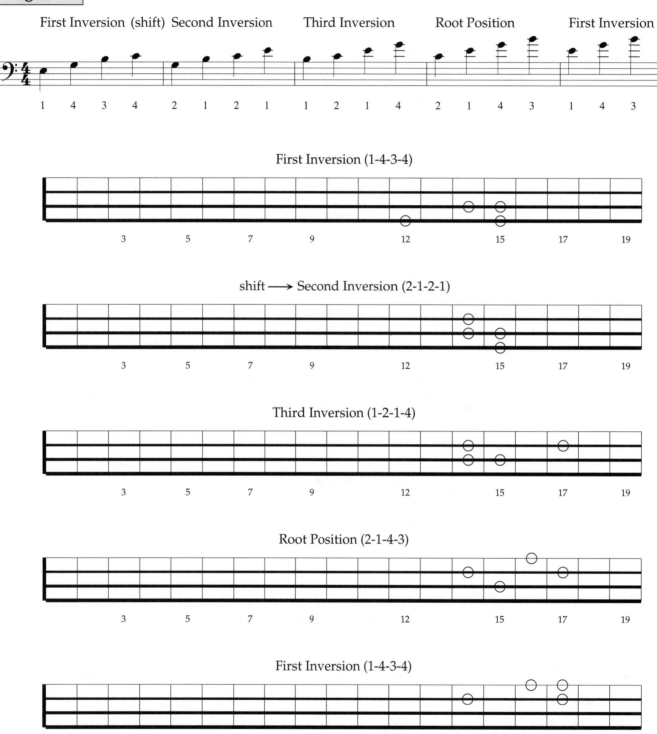

Figure 3

First Inversion (shift) Second Inversion Third Inversion Root Position First Inversion

1 4 3 4   2 1 2 1   1 2 1 4   2 1 4 3   1 4 3 4

First Inversion (1-4-3-4)

shift → Second Inversion (2-1-2-1)

Third Inversion (1-2-1-4)

Root Position (2-1-4-3)

First Inversion (1-4-3-4)

Review the three areas of the neck where the arpeggios for C major seventh are found. Only four shapes should be used. Play the arpeggios so they sound smooth and connected; make sure there is no pause or interruption of the line when the shift between first and second inversion occurs. Play them all repeatedly until each is memorized.

Again using C as the root, play each version of the major seventh arpeggio beginning on the E string. The first one is second inversion at the third fret. Next is the third inversion at the seventh fret. Follow that with the root position at the eighth fret. Notice that no shift occurs between the third inversion and root position. At the twelfth fret, play first inversion and then conclude with second inversion at the fifteenth fret. Play this arpeggio so that the shifts are quick and smooth, sounding as if it was played in one position.

Figure 4 is played with each version beginning on the E string.

Figure 4

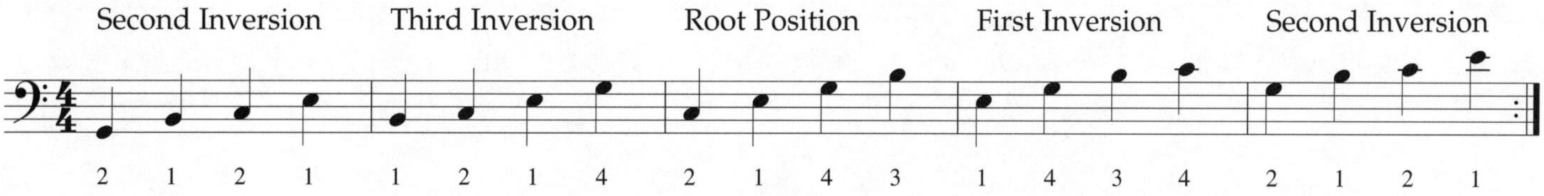

Second Inversion   Third Inversion   Root Position   First Inversion   Second Inversion

2 1 2 1   1 2 1 4   2 1 4 3   1 4 3 4   2 1 2 1

Second Inversion (1-2-1-2)

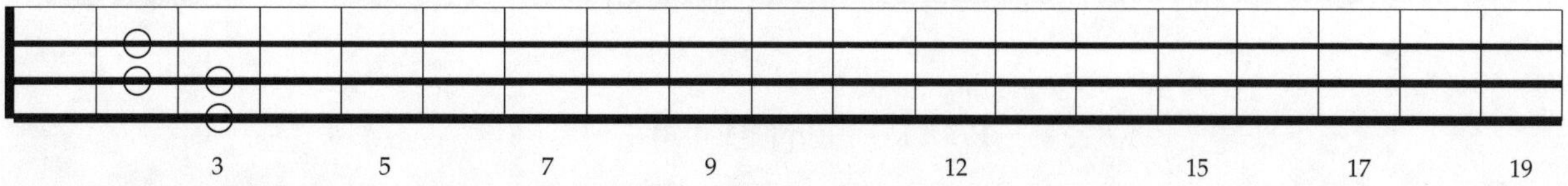

Third Inversion (1-2-1-4)

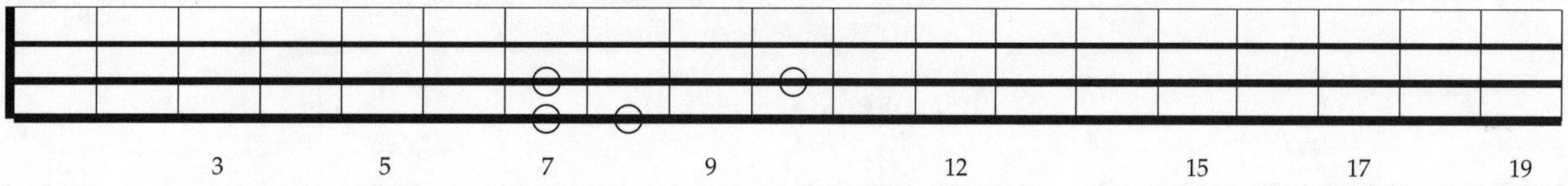

Root Position (2-1-4-3)

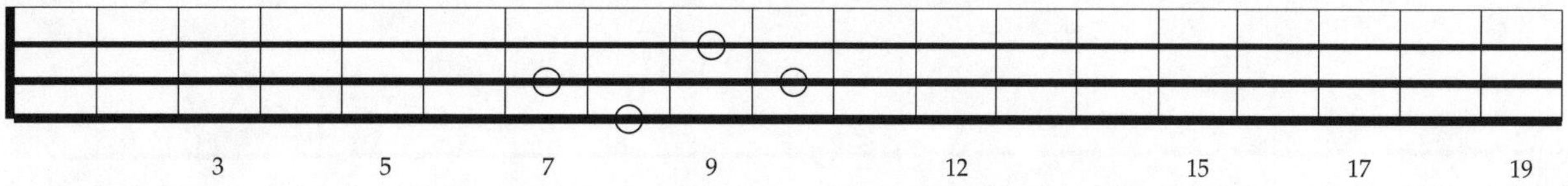

First Inversion (1-4-3-4)

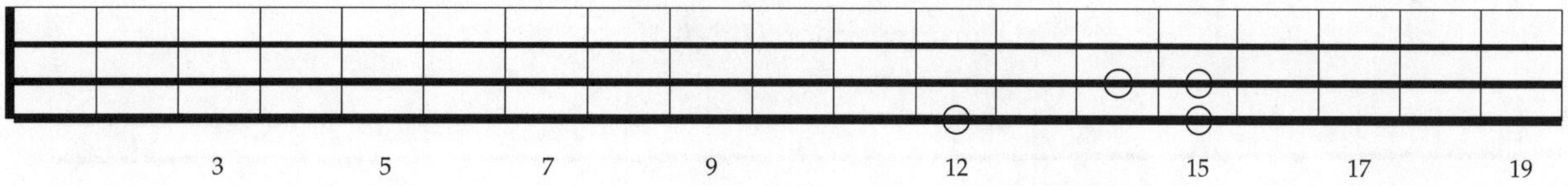

Second Inversion (2-1-2-1)

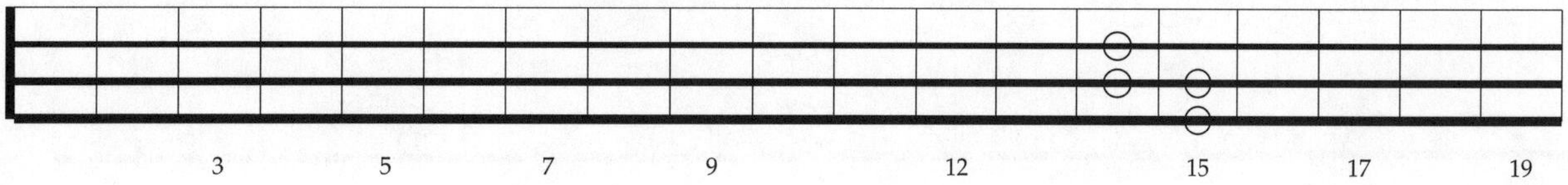

Now move this exercise to the A string, starting with the third inversion at the second fret. Root position at the third fret is next—no shift is necessary. Play first inversion at the seventh fret, second inversion at the tenth, and then repeat third inversion and root position at the twelfth and thirteenth frets.

Figure 5 is played with each version beginning on the A string.

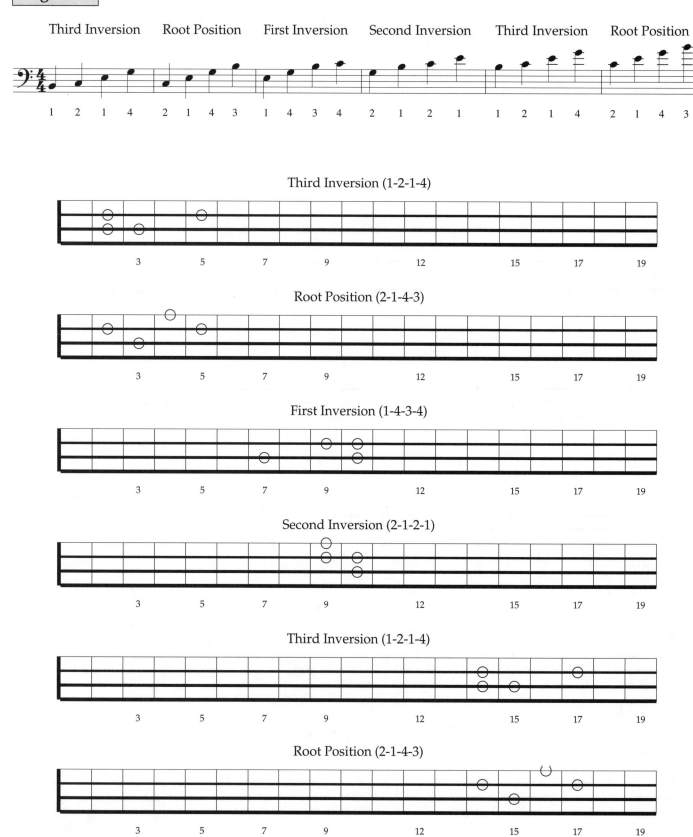

After a review of C major seventh, move on to the other root names. G and D have been included as examples. Use the two systems of study discussed: first study each chord in one area at a time, then play each version beginning from the same string and in a different position. Always play the full range of the chord. Remember that both exercises share the same four fingering shapes for all root names and locations.

G MAJOR SEVENTH (Gmaj7)

Play the next three figures each in one area of the neck.

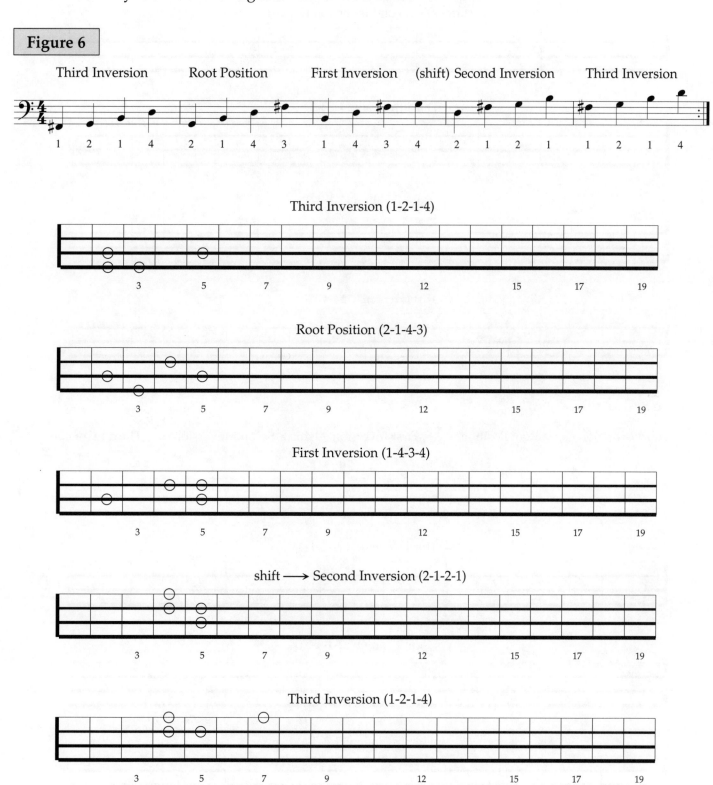

Figure 7

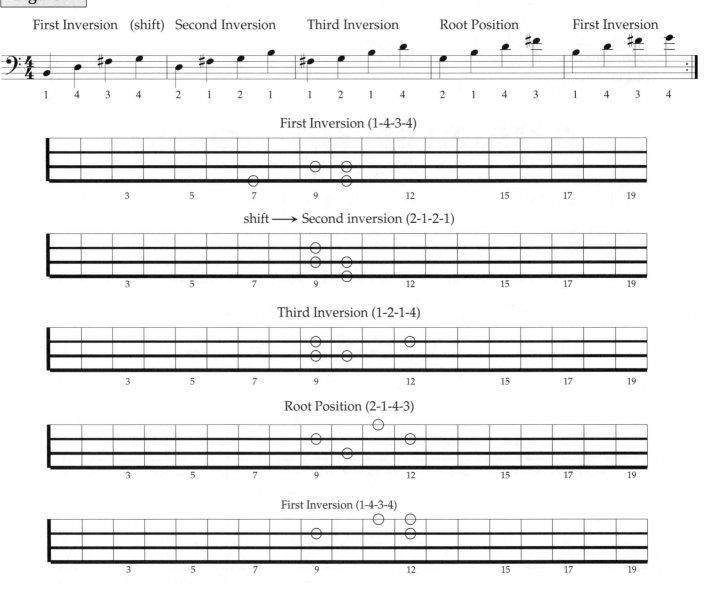

Figure 8

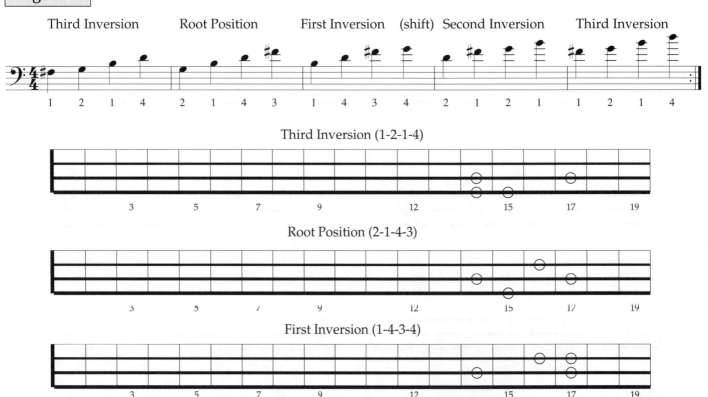

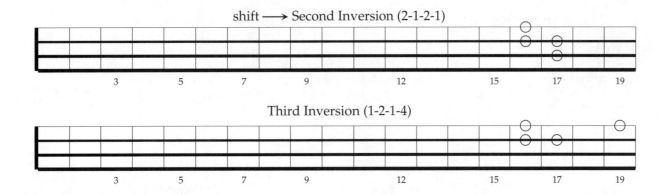

shift ⟶ Second Inversion (2-1-2-1)

Third Inversion (1-2-1-4)

Now play each version beginning on the E string.

Figure 9

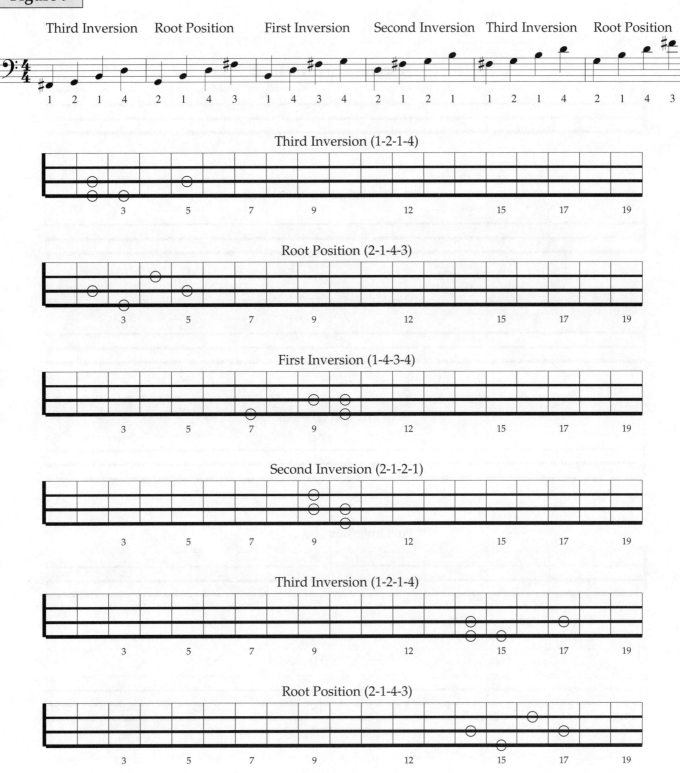

Third Inversion (1-2-1-4)

Root Position (2-1-4-3)

First Inversion (1-4-3-4)

Second Inversion (2-1-2-1)

Third Inversion (1-2-1-4)

Root Position (2-1-4-3)

Now play each version beginning on the A string.

Figure 10

First Inversion   Second Inversion   Third Inversion

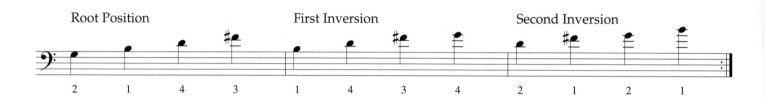

Root Position   First Inversion   Second Inversion

First Inversion (1-4-3-4)

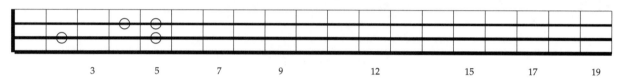

Second Inversion (2-1-2-1)

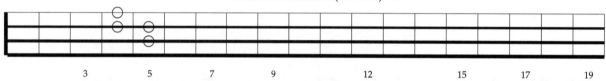

Third Inversion (1-2-1-4)

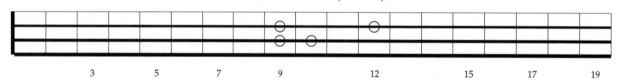

Root Position (2-1-4-3)

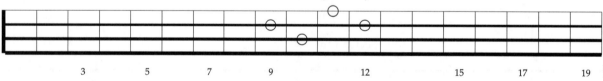

First Inversion (1-4-3-4)

Second inversion (2-1-2-1)

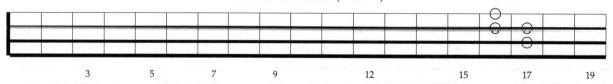

D MAJOR SEVENTH (Dmaj7)

Play the next three figures each in one area of the neck.

Figure 11

First Inversion   Second Inversion   Third Inversion   Root Position   First Inversion

1   4   3   4   2   1   2   1   1   2   1   4   2   1   4   3   1   4   3   4

First Inversion (1-4-3-4)

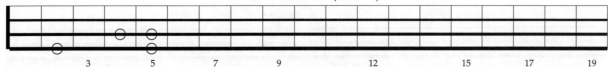

3   5   7   9   12   15   17   19

shift ⟶ Second Inversion (2-1-2-1)

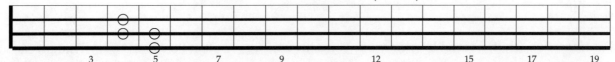

3   5   7   9   12   15   17   19

Third Inversion (1-2-1-4)

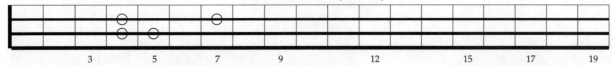

3   5   7   9   12   15   17   19

Root Position (2-1-4-3)

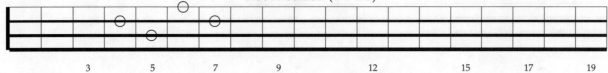

3   5   7   9   12   15   17   19

First Inversion (1-4-3-4)

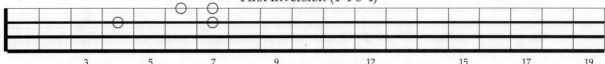

3   5   7   9   12   15   17   19

Figure 12

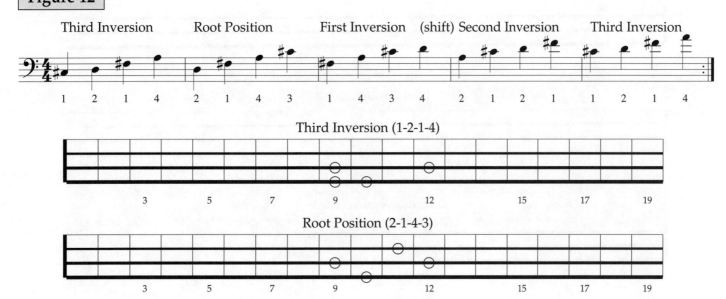

Third Inversion   Root Position   First Inversion   (shift) Second Inversion   Third Inversion

1   2   1   4   2   1   4   3   1   4   3   4   2   1   2   1   1   2   1   4

Third Inversion (1-2-1-4)

3   5   7   9   12   15   17   19

Root Position (2-1-4-3)

3   5   7   9   12   15   17   19

First Inversion (1-4-3-4)

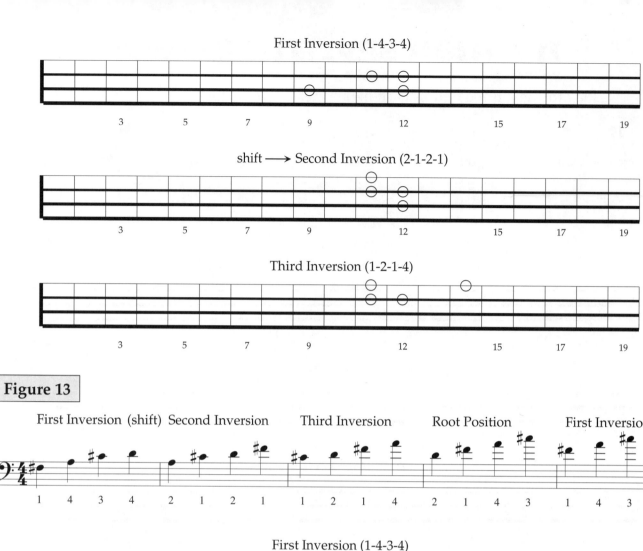

shift ⟶ Second Inversion (2-1-2-1)

Third Inversion (1-2-1-4)

Figure 13

First Inversion (shift) Second Inversion   Third Inversion   Root Position   First Inversion

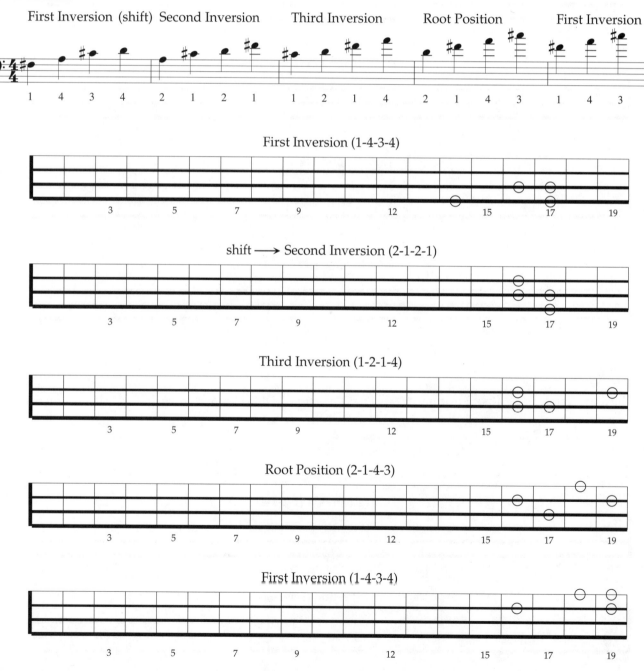

First Inversion (1-4-3-4)

shift ⟶ Second Inversion (2-1-2-1)

Third Inversion (1-2-1-4)

Root Position (2-1-4-3)

First Inversion (1-4-3-4)

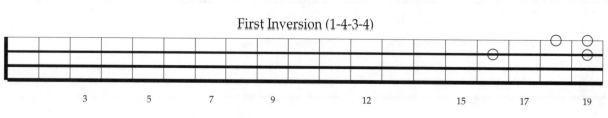

Play each version beginning on the E string.

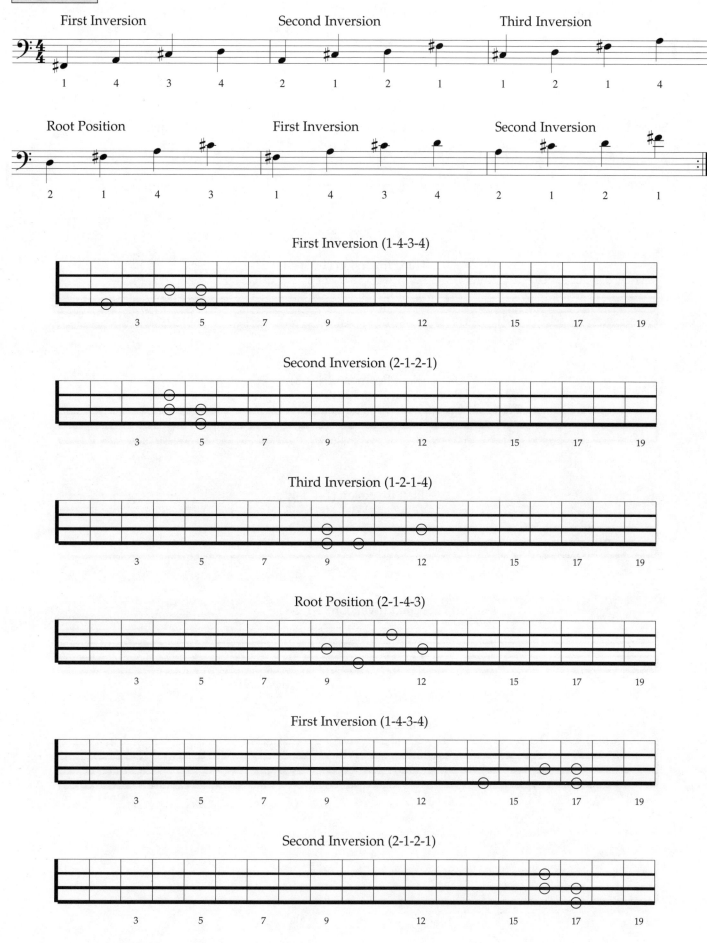

Figure 14

First Inversion   Second Inversion   Third Inversion

1   4   3   4   2   1   2   1   1   2   1   4

Root Position   First Inversion   Second Inversion

2   1   4   3   1   4   3   4   2   1   2   1

First Inversion (1-4-3-4)

Second Inversion (2-1-2-1)

Third Inversion (1-2-1-4)

Root Position (2-1-4-3)

First Inversion (1-4-3-4)

Second Inversion (2-1-2-1)

Play each version beginning on the A string.

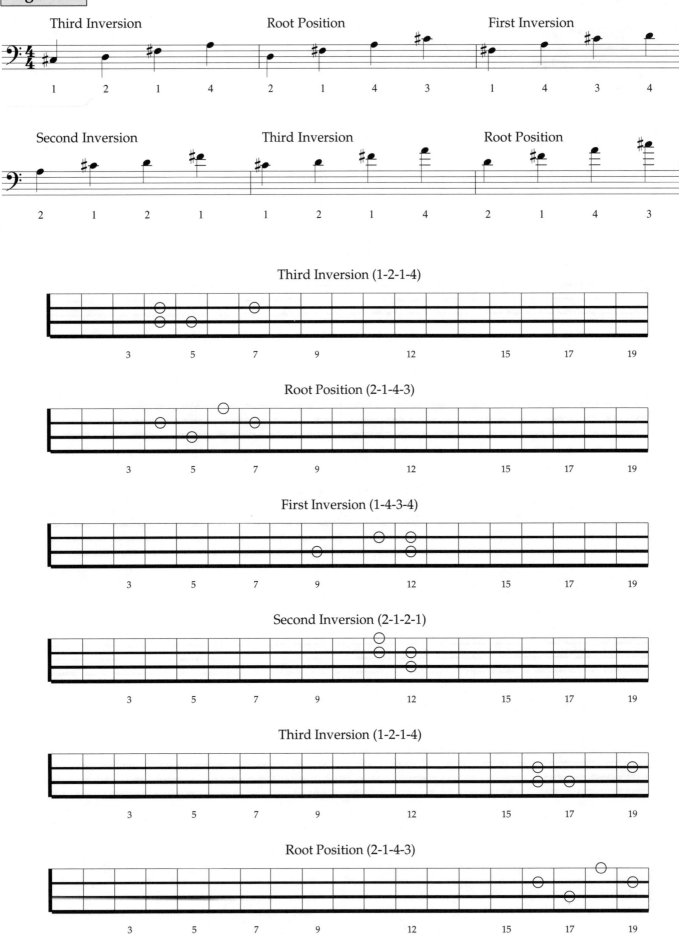

Figure 15

Third Inversion

Root Position

First Inversion

1   2   1   4   2   1   4   3   1   4   3   4

Second Inversion

Third Inversion

Root Position

2   1   2   1   1   2   1   4   2   1   4   3

Third Inversion (1-2-1-4)

3   5   7   9   12   15   17   19

Root Position (2-1-4-3)

3   5   7   9   12   15   17   19

First Inversion (1-4-3-4)

3   5   7   9   12   15   17   19

Second Inversion (2-1-2-1)

3   5   7   9   12   15   17   19

Third Inversion (1-2-1-4)

3   5   7   9   12   15   17   19

Root Position (2-1-4-3)

3   5   7   9   12   15   17   19

6. DOMINANT SEVENTH

Like the major seventh chord, a dominant seventh chord (dom7 or 7) occurs in the harmonization of the major scale. As the major seventh chord was a major triad with a major seventh interval added, the dominant seventh chord is a major triad with a *minor* seventh added.

Notice that only one note has changed (the seventh) between the spelling of this chord and the major seventh chord. However, in order to study this arpeggio, four new shapes are necessary. Root position, first inversion, and second inversion are very similar to the major seventh chord, but the third inversion is quite different. Each version will have one shape only, consistent among all root names and locations on the neck. Always start with the lowest possible version (no open strings) and play the full range of the arpeggio in each position.

Using C as the example, root position is spelled C–E–G–B♭, first inversion is E–G–B♭–C, second inversion is G–B♭–C–E, and third inversion is B♭–C–E–G. Examples with the root G and D are included, but all root names should be practiced to gain the maximum benefit from this study.

This method teaches you a very systematic way of learning arpeggios, but there are alternate shapes which may appear more efficient. In a performance situation, these other fingerings may be your preference.

Guidelines for Dominant Seventh Chords

Four spellings	Notes
Root position	(1-3-5-♭7)
First inversion	(3-5-♭7-1)
Second inversion	(5-♭7-1-3)
Third inversion	(♭7-1-3-5)

One fingering shape per spelling, consistent among all root names and locations on the neck.

	Fingering
Root position	2-1-4-2
First inversion	1-4-2-4
Second inversion	4-2-4-3
Third inversion	2-4-3-1

No open strings included in fingering shape.

Arpeggiations begin with the lowest possible spelling on the fretboard.

No position shifts during the arpeggiation of a spelling—only between spellings.

Begin C dominant seventh (or C7) with the second inversion (third fret G on the E string) and after a five fret shift (second finger up to B♭), play the third inversion. Although this may seem awkward and unnecessary, it is consistent with our guidelines of no open strings or shifts within a spelling. During a performance, there might be a more efficient choice.

To play root position, shift back to the first area (second finger C on the A string). Finish the arpeggio in that area with the first inversion.

C SEVENTH (C7)

Figure 1

Second Inversion   (shift)   Third Inversion   (shift)   Root Position   First Inversion

4   2   4   3   2   4   3   1   2   1   4   2   1   4   2   4

Second Inversion (4-2-4-3)

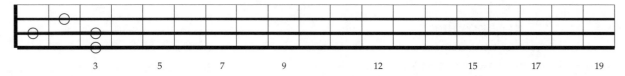

shift ⟶ Third Inversion (2-4-3-1)

Root Position (2-1-4-2) ⟵ shift

First Inversion (1-4-2-4)

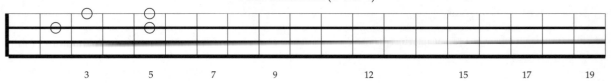

The next area for C seventh begins with the third inversion (sixth fret B♭ on the E string), followed this time with a two-fret shift up the E string, where root position is played. Next is the first inversion and second inversion. Notice that if we ignore our guideline of no shifting during a version, a repeat of third inversion is available.

Figure 2

Third Inversion   (shift)   Root Position   First Inversion   Second Inversion

2   4   3   1   2   1   4   2   1   4   2   4   4   2   4   3

Third Inversion (2-4-3-1)

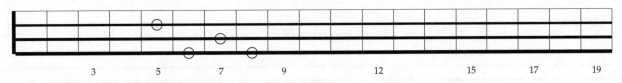

3   5   7   9   12   15   17   19

shift ⟶ Root Position (2-1-4-2)

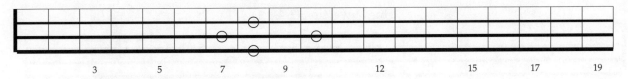

3   5   7   9   12   15   17   19

First Inversion (1-4-2-4)

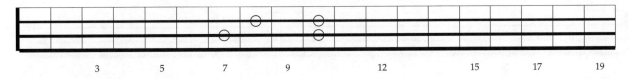

3   5   7   9   12   15   17   19

Second Inversion (4-2-4-3)

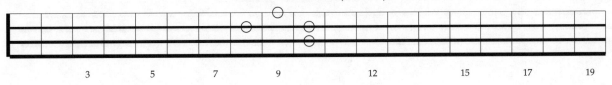

3   5   7   9   12   15   17   19

To cover the last area for C seventh, begin the arpeggio with first inversion at the twelfth fret. Follow that with second and third inversions. All three are played without any shifts. Make a two-fret shift (second finger C on the A string) to finish with root position and a repeat of first inversion.

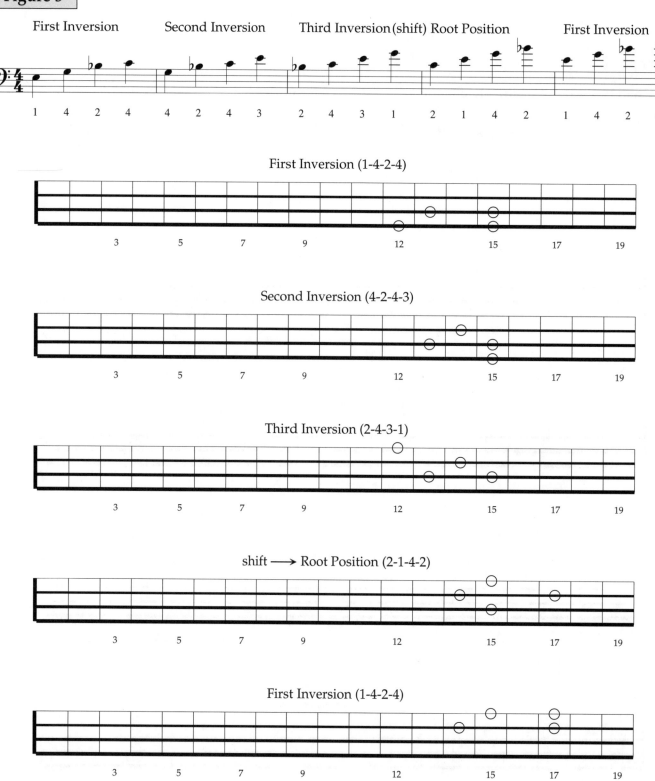

Figure 3

Review the three areas on the neck where C seventh is arpeggiated and play repeatedly until all the shifts are smooth, and the spellings and sounds are memorized.

In this section, play each version of the dominant seventh chord beginning from the E string only. Arpeggios will be played up the neck rather than in one area. Using C seventh as the example, begin with the second inversion at the third fret. Next is the third inversion at the sixth fret, root position at the eighth fret, first inversion at the twelfth fret and a repeat of the second inversion at the fifteenth fret. Play repeatedly until all shifts are smooth and uninterrupted.

Play each version beginning on the E string.

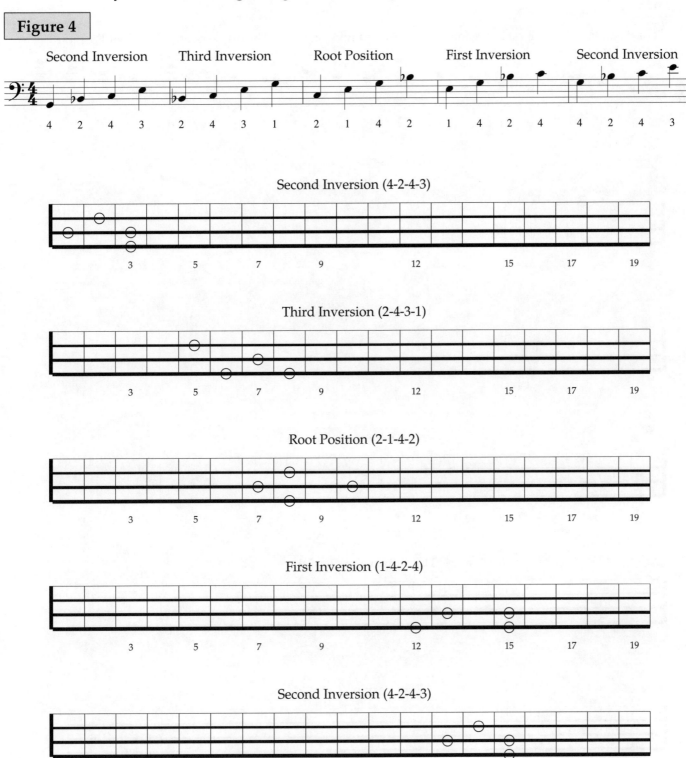

Then move the arpeggio to the A string and play each version starting there. Root position begins at the third fret. Follow up with first inversion at the seventh fret, second inversion at the tenth fret, third inversion at the thirteenth fret, and a repeat of root position at the fifteenth fret. The arpeggio should sound as if it were played in one position.

Play each version beginning on the A string.

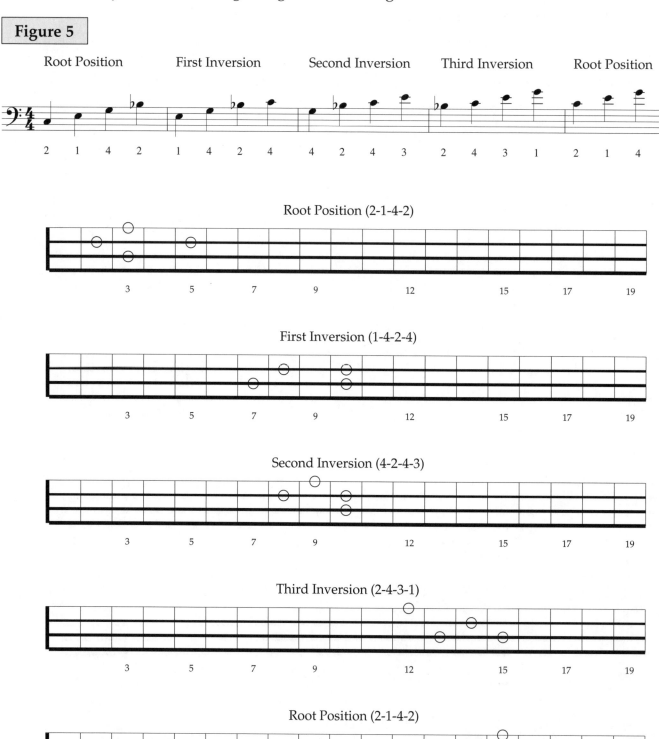

Figure 5

After a review of C seventh, use the arpeggio method to study all the root names. G seventh and D seventh have been included as examples. Play each root name until the spellings and neck locations are memorized.

G SEVENTH (G7)

Play the next three figures each in one area of the neck.

Figure 6

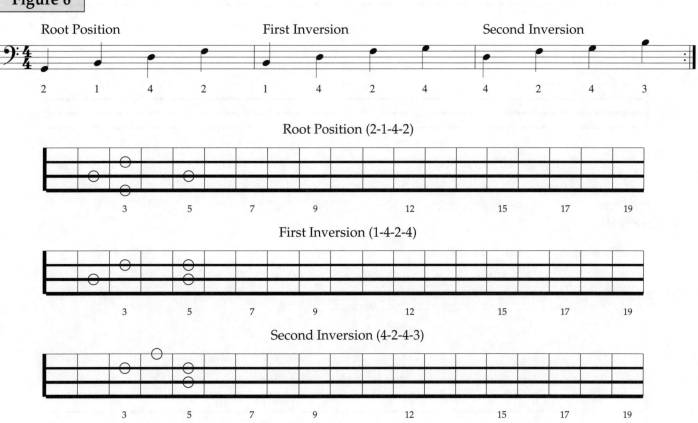

Figure 7

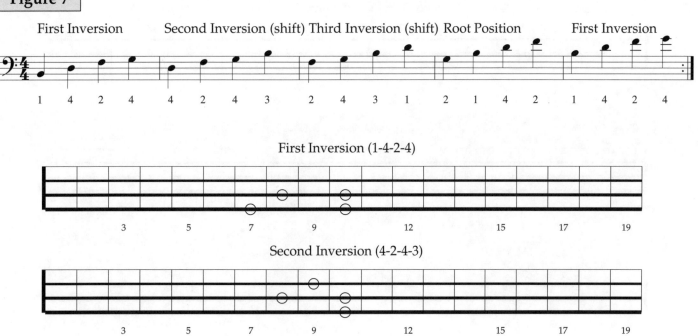

Third Inversion (2-4-3-1)

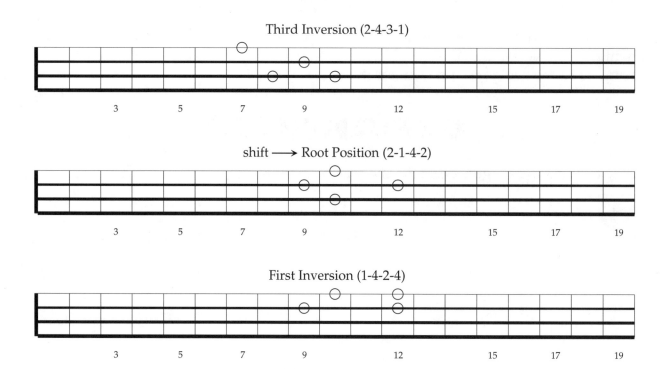

shift → Root Position (2-1-4-2)

First Inversion (1-4-2-4)

Figure 8

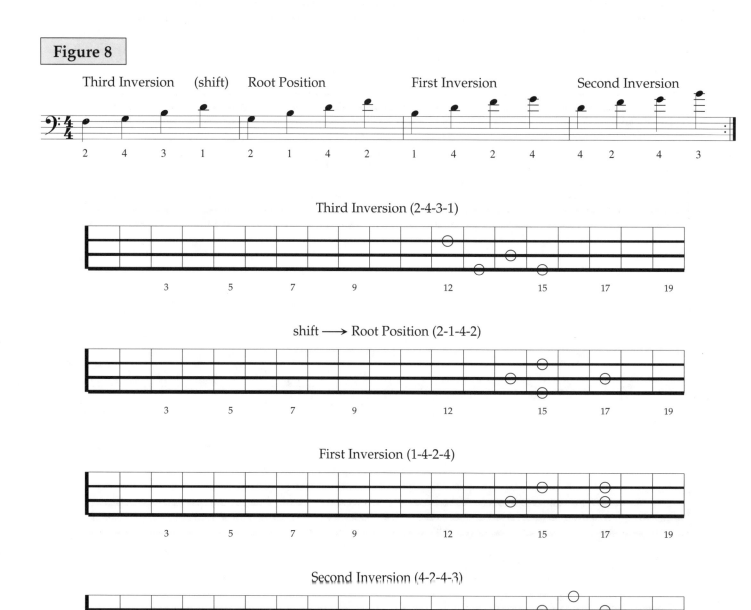

Third Inversion   (shift)   Root Position   First Inversion   Second Inversion

2   4   3   1   2   1   4   2   1   4   2   4   4   2   4   3

Third Inversion (2-4-3-1)

shift → Root Position (2-1-4-2)

First Inversion (1-4-2-4)

Second Inversion (4-2-4-3)

Play each version beginning on the E string.

Figure 9

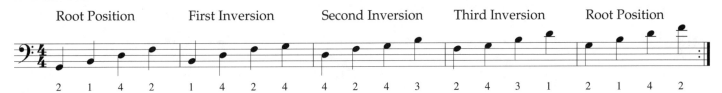

Root Position   First Inversion   Second Inversion   Third Inversion   Root Position

2 1 4 2   1 4 2 4   4 2 4 3   2 4 3 1   2 1 4 2

Root Position (2-1-4-2)

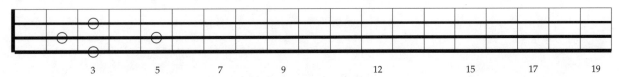

First Inversion (1-4-2-4)

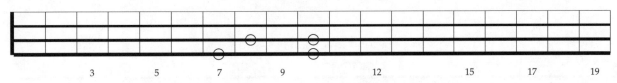

Second Inversion (4-2-4-3)

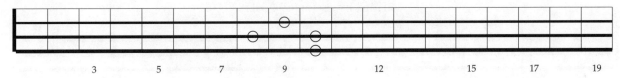

Third Inversion (2-4-3-1)

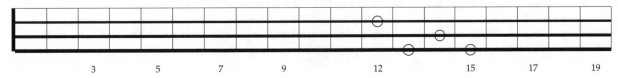

Root Position (2-1-4-2)

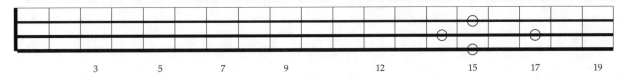

Play each version beginning on the A string.

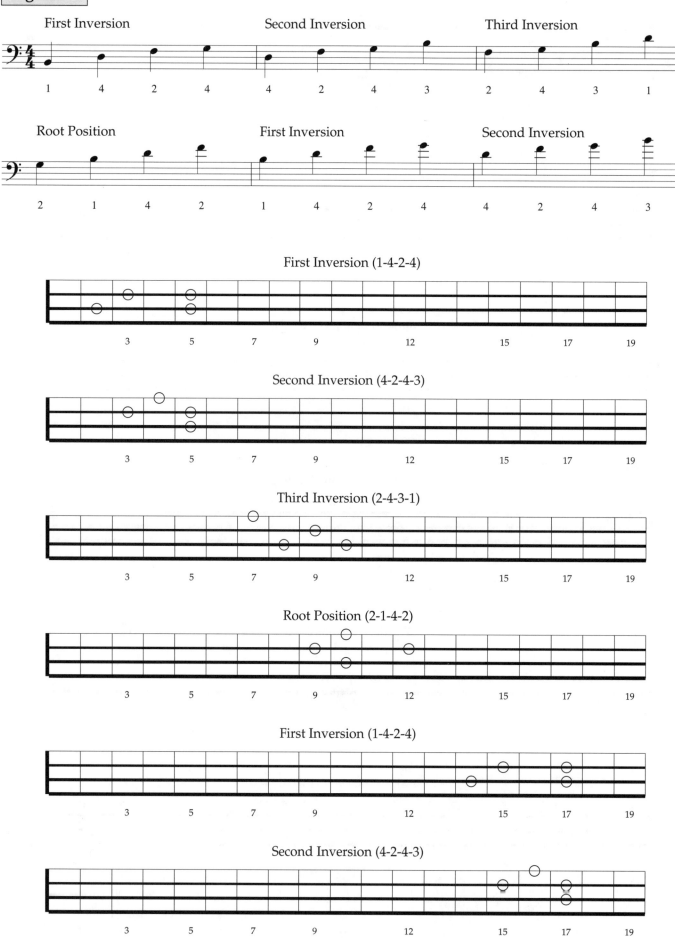

D SEVENTH (D7)

Play the next three figures each in one area of the neck.

Figure 11

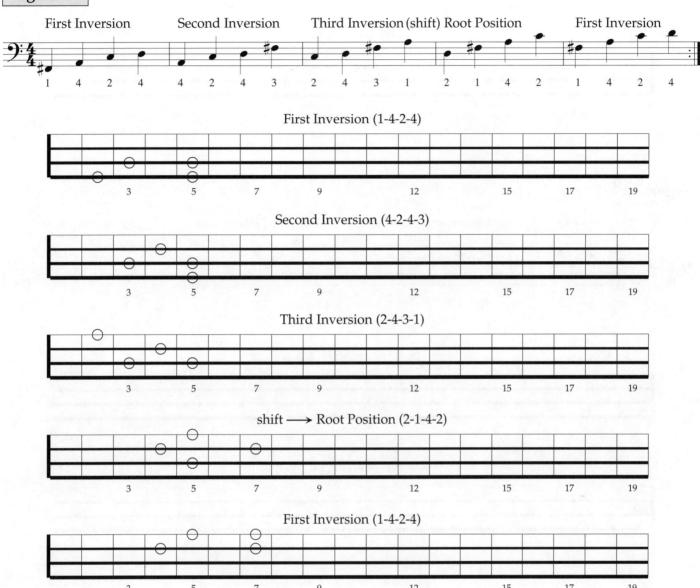

First Inversion   Second Inversion   Third Inversion (shift) Root Position   First Inversion

1   4   2   4   4   2   4   3   2   4   3   1   2   1   4   2   1   4   2   4

First Inversion (1-4-2-4)

Second Inversion (4-2-4-3)

Third Inversion (2-4-3-1)

shift ⟶ Root Position (2-1-4-2)

First Inversion (1-4-2-4)

Figure 12

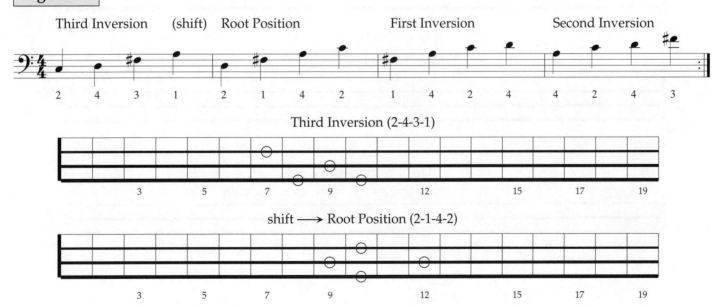

Third Inversion   (shift)   Root Position   First Inversion   Second Inversion

2   4   3   1   2   1   4   2   1   4   2   4   4   2   4   3

Third Inversion (2-4-3-1)

shift ⟶ Root Position (2-1-4-2)

First Inversion (1-4-2-4)

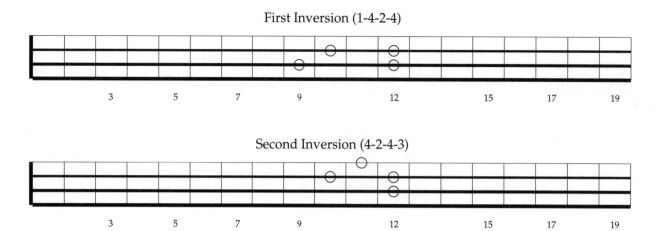

Second Inversion (4-2-4-3)

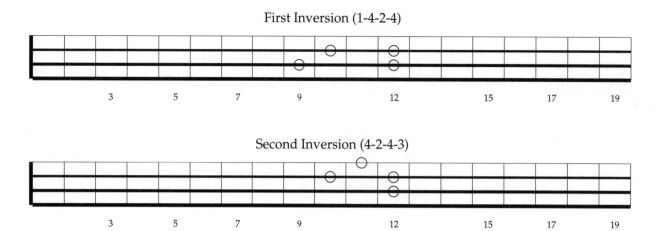

Figure 13

First Inversion   Second Inversion   Third Inversion (shift) Root Position   First Inversion

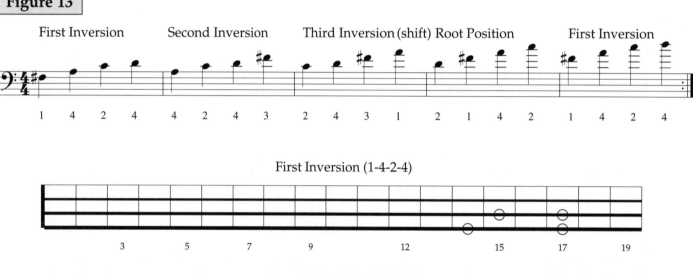

First Inversion (1-4-2-4)

Second Inversion (4-2-4-3)

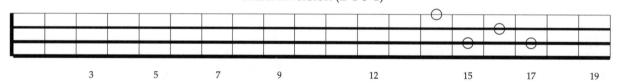

Third Inversion (2-4-3-1)

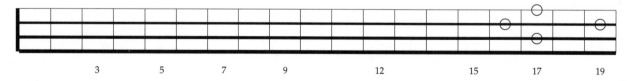

shift ⟶ Root Position (2-1-4-2)

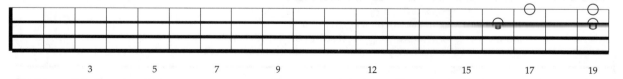

First Inversion (1-4-2-4)

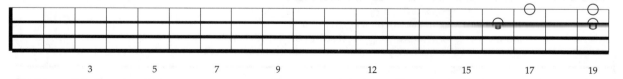

Play each version beginning on the E string.

Figure 14

First Inversion   Second Inversion   Third Inversion

Root Position   First Inversion   Second Inversion

First Inversion (1-4-2-4)

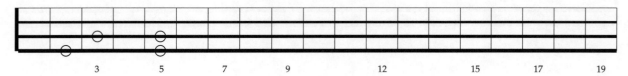

Second Inversion (4-2-4-3)

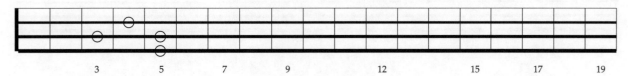

Third Inversion (2-4-3-1)

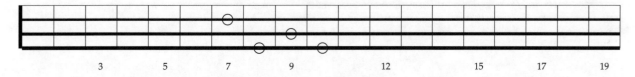

Root Position (2-1-4-2)

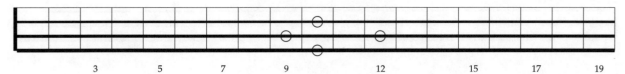

First Inversion (1-4-2-4)

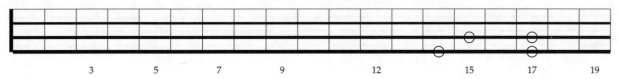

Second Inversion (4-2-4-3)

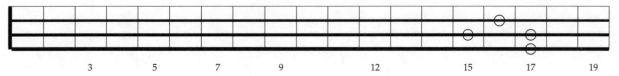

Now play each version beginning on the A string.

Figure 15

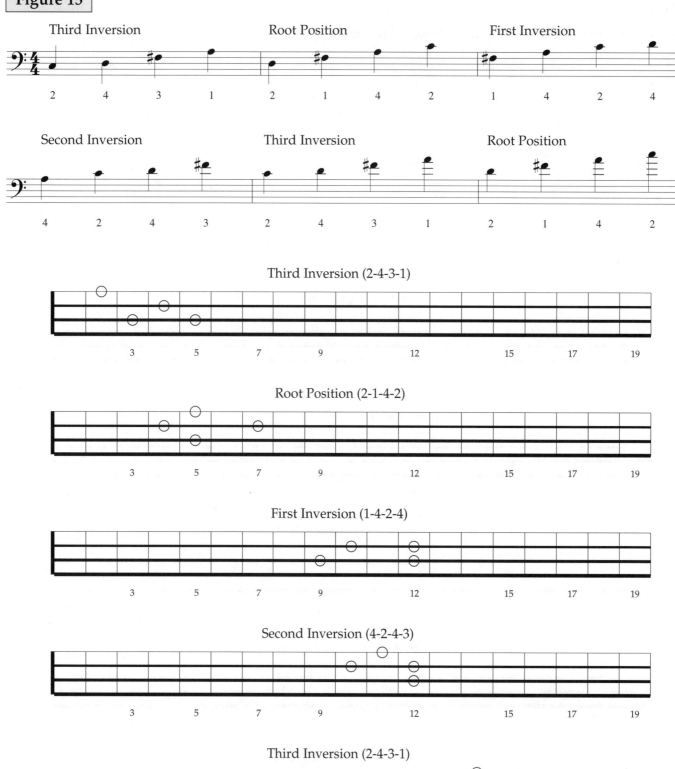

Third Inversion (2-4-3-1)

Root Position (2-1-4-2)

First Inversion (1-4-2-4)

Second Inversion (4-2-4-3)

Third Inversion (2-4-3-1)

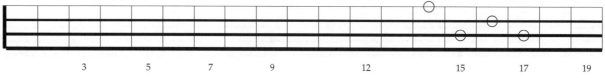

Root Position (2-1-4-2)

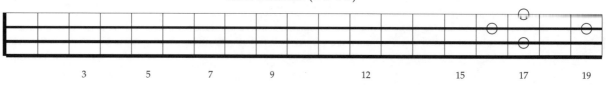

7. MINOR SEVENTH

Using the same method, we will continue arpeggiations with minor seventh (m7) chords. A minor seventh chord is a minor triad with a minor seventh interval added. The spelling for C minor seventh in root position is C–E♭–G–B♭. First inversion is spelled E♭–G–B♭–C, second inversion is G–B♭–C–E♭, and third inversion is B♭–C–E♭–G.

Each version will have one shape regardless of the root name or location on the neck. Once again, it may appear that alternate shapes provide a better fingering path. It will be beneficial to explore these options later.

As before, there is a set of guidelines to follow to quickly learn the shapes for all possible root names. Practice each root name repeatedly, but play several root names at each practice session, so that the consistency of shapes is memorized. The spelling of each version and neck location is equally important and should not be overlooked.

When practicing each arpeggio, start with the lowest possible spelling and play the full range of the arpeggio.

Guidelines for Minor Seventh Chords

Four spellings	Notes
Root position	(1-♭3-5-♭7)
First inversion	(♭3-5-♭7-1)
Second inversion	(5-♭7-1-♭3)
Third inversion	(♭7-1-♭3-5)

One fingering shape per spelling, consistent among all root names and locations on the neck.

	Fingering
Root position	1-4-3-1
First inversion	2-1-4-1
Second inversion	1-4-1-4
Third inversion	4-1-4 3

No open strings included in fingering shape.

Arpeggiations begin with the lowest possible spelling on the fretboard.

No position shifts during the arpeggiation of a spelling—only between spellings.

Start C minor seventh with the second inversion at the third fret of the E string. Without shifting, play the third inversion and root position. First inversion and a repeat of second inversion are next, and require a two-fret ascending shift.

C MINOR SEVENTH (Cm7)

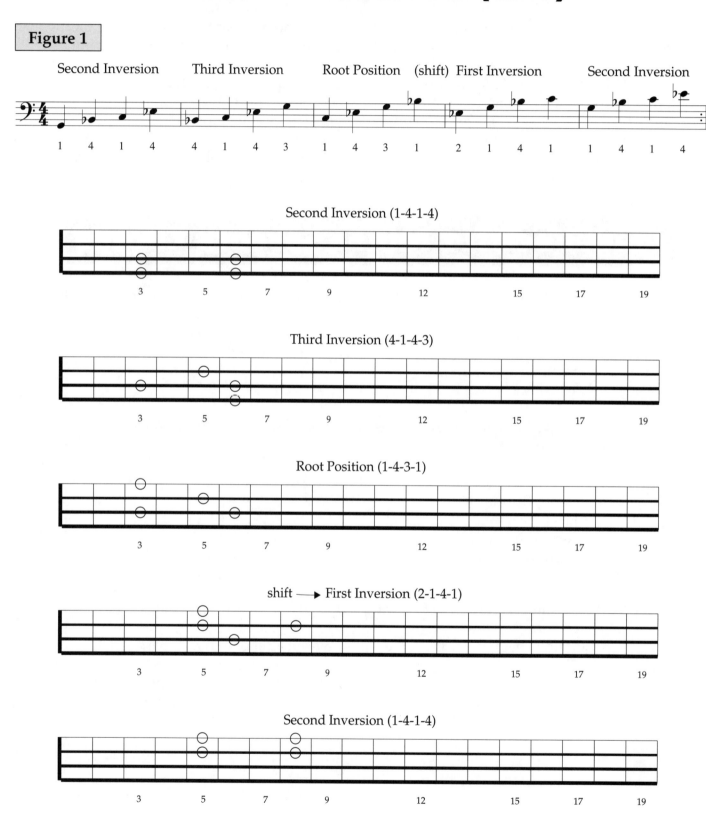

Moving to the next area, start in root position at the eighth fret (C on the E string). Make a two-fret shift and play first, second, and third inversions in a single position.

Figure 2

Root Position · First Inversion · Second Inversion · Third Inversion

1 4 3 1 2 1 4 1 1 4 1 4 4 1 4 3

Root Position (1-4-3-1)

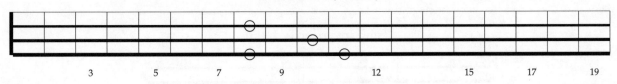

3   5   7   9   12   15   17   19

shift ⟶ First Inversion (2-1-4-1)

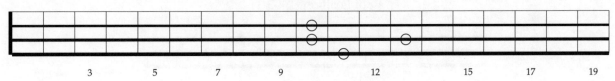

3   5   7   9   12   15   17   19

Second Inversion (1-4-1-4)

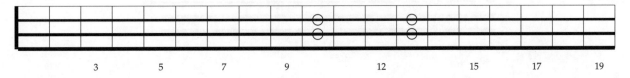

3   5   7   9   12   15   17   19

Third Inversion (4-1-4-3)

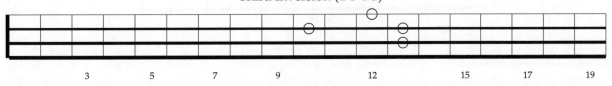

3   5   7   9   12   15   17   19

The last area begins with the second inversion at the fifteenth fret. Play third inversion and root position before making a two-fret shift for first inversion and a repeat of second inversion.

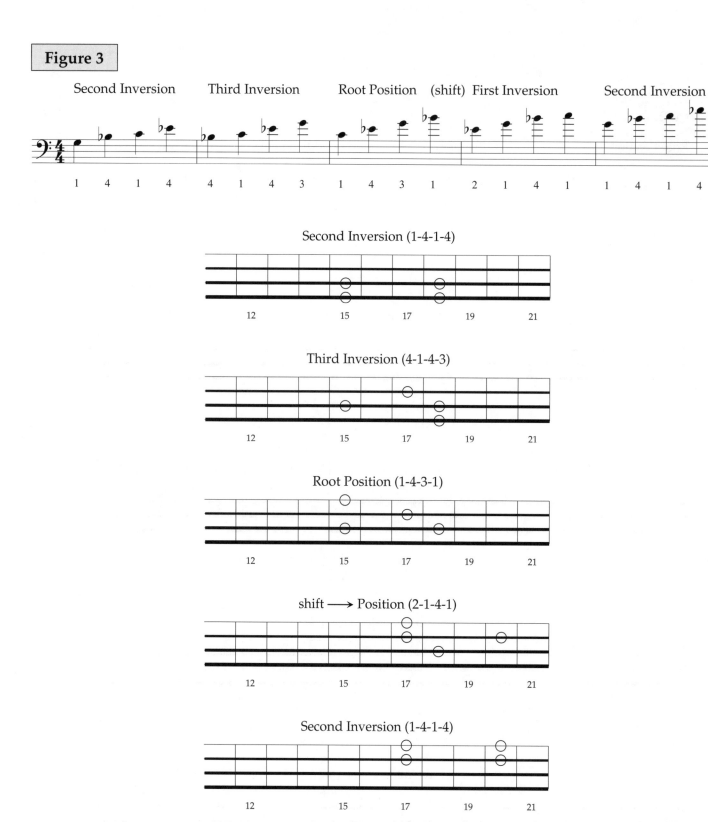

Figure 3

Review each of the three areas on the neck where the arpeggio was played. Only four shapes should be used. It is important to memorize the spelling and sound of each version and to be familiar with arpeggio locations.

Continue with minor seventh chords, playing each version starting on the E string only. For C minor seventh, begin with the second inversion at the third fret and follow that with third inversion at the sixth fret. Root position is next at the eighth fret, then first inversion at the eleventh fret, and finish with a repeat of second inversion at the fifteenth fret. Each spelling will of course have the same fingering shapes learned in the first section, and the entire arpeggio should sound connected as if there were no shifts.

Play each version beginning on the E string.

Figure 4

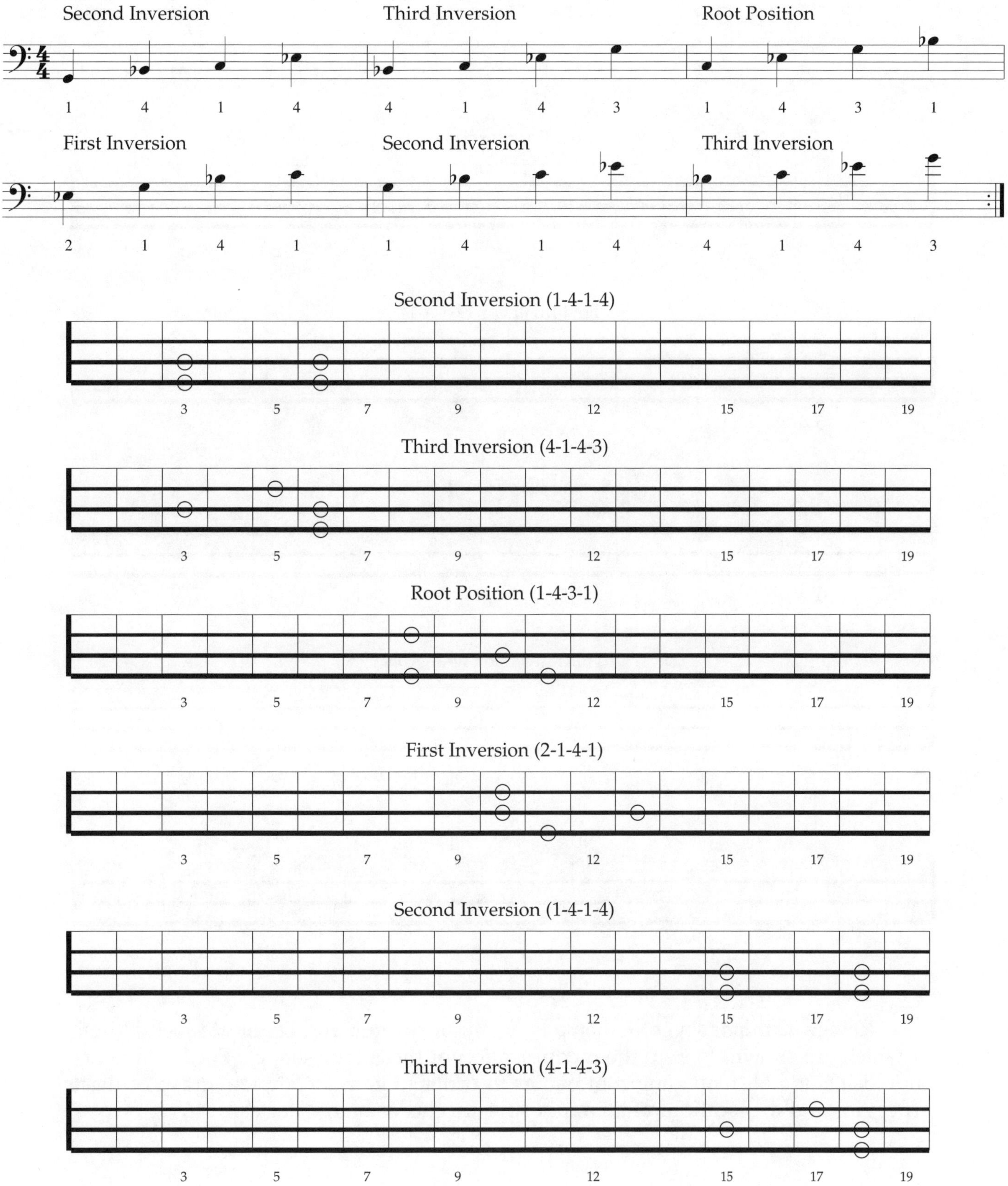

Second Inversion (1-4-1-4)

Third Inversion (4-1-4-3)

Root Position (1-4-3-1)

First Inversion (2-1-4-1)

Second Inversion (1-4-1-4)

Third Inversion (4-1-4-3)

Now repeat the method from the A string starting with root position at the third fret. Next play first inversion at the sixth fret, second inversion at the tenth fret, third inversion at the thirteenth fret, and a repeat of root position at the fifteenth fret. Remember to use the same four shapes and work for smooth, connected shifts.

Play each version beginning on the A string.

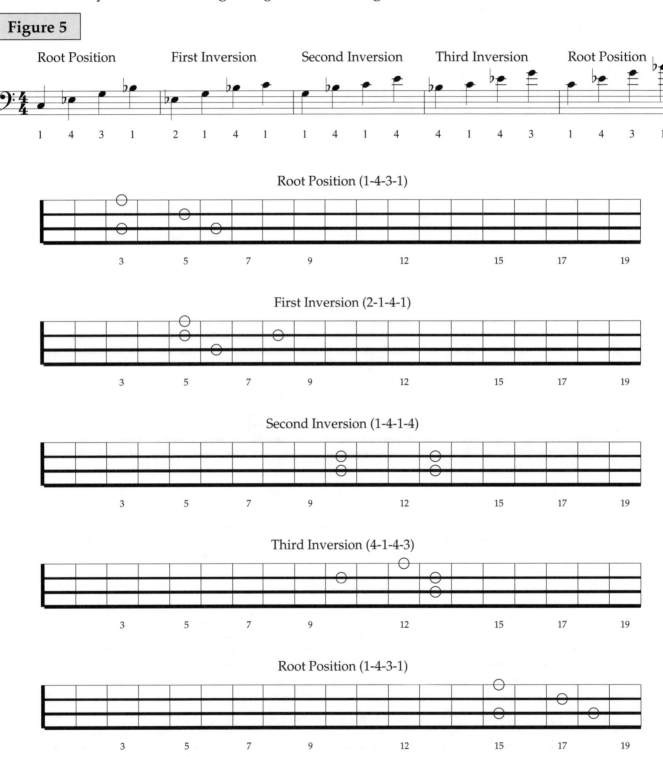

Figure 5

Root Position First Inversion Second Inversion Third Inversion Root Position

Root Position (1-4-3-1)

First Inversion (2-1-4-1)

Second Inversion (1-4-1-4)

Third Inversion (4-1-4-3)

Root Position (1-4-3-1)

Review C minor seventh, then play G minor seventh and D minor seventh (both of which are shown) to help the memorization of these four shapes. Further practice should include all remaining root names in order to gain a complete grasp of these arpeggios and the locations of all minor seventh chords on the neck.

G MINOR SEVENTH (Gm7)

Play the next three figures each in one area of the neck.

Figure 6

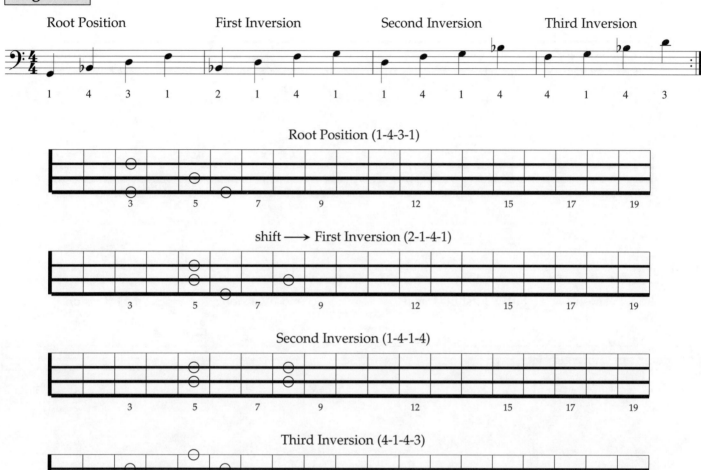

Root Position   First Inversion   Second Inversion   Third Inversion

Root Position (1-4-3-1)

shift ⟶ First Inversion (2-1-4-1)

Second Inversion (1-4-1-4)

Third Inversion (4-1-4-3)

Figure 7

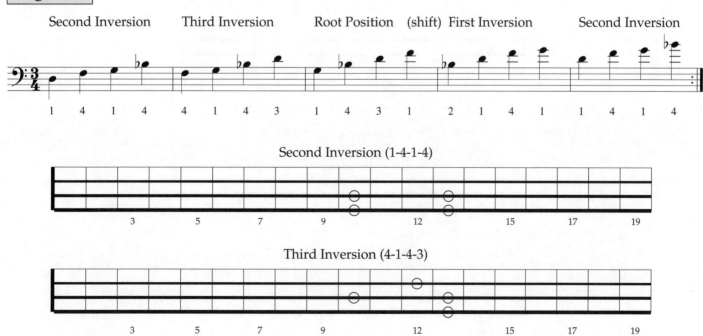

Second Inversion   Third Inversion   Root Position   (shift) First Inversion   Second Inversion

Second Inversion (1-4-1-4)

Third Inversion (4-1-4-3)

Root Position (1-4-3-1)

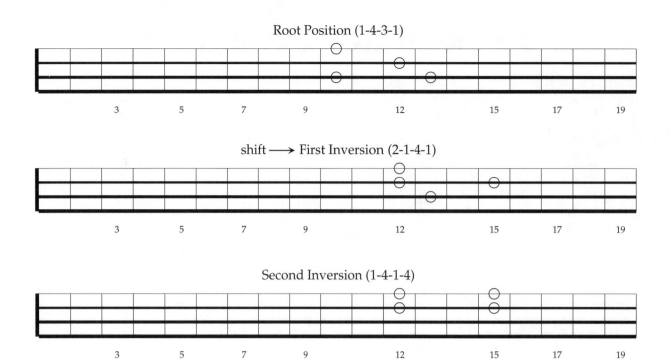

shift ⟶ First Inversion (2-1-4-1)

Second Inversion (1-4-1-4)

Figure 8

 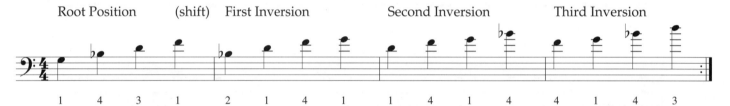

Root Position	(shift)	First Inversion	Second Inversion	Third Inversion

1 4 3 1 2 1 4 1 1 4 1 4 4 1 4 3

Root Position (1-4-3-1)

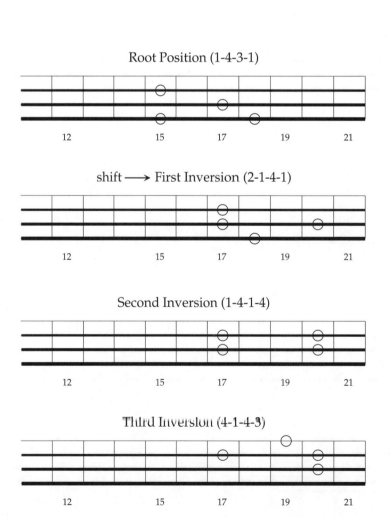

shift ⟶ First Inversion (2-1-4-1)

Second Inversion (1-4-1-4)

Third Inversion (4-1-4-3)

Now play each version beginning on the E string.

Figure 9

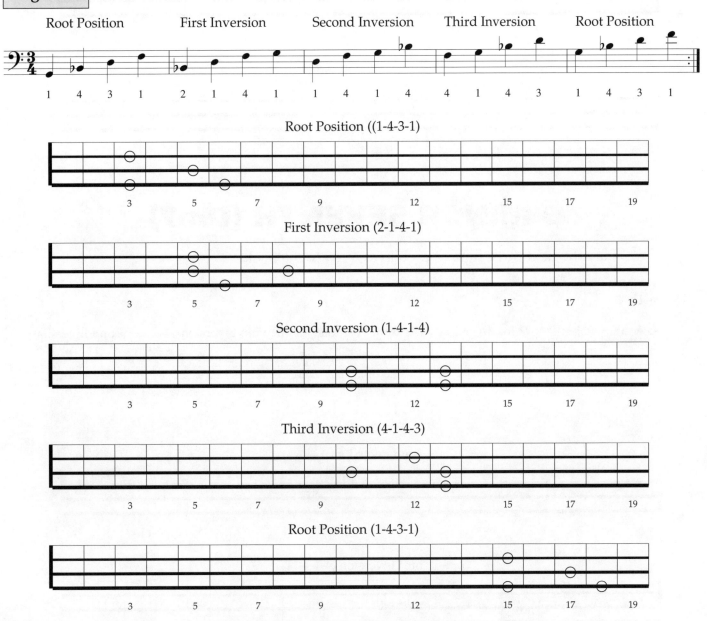

Root Position ((1-4-3-1)

First Inversion (2-1-4-1)

Second Inversion (1-4-1-4)

Third Inversion (4-1-4-3)

Root Position (1-4-3-1)

Now play each version beginning on the A string.

Figure 10

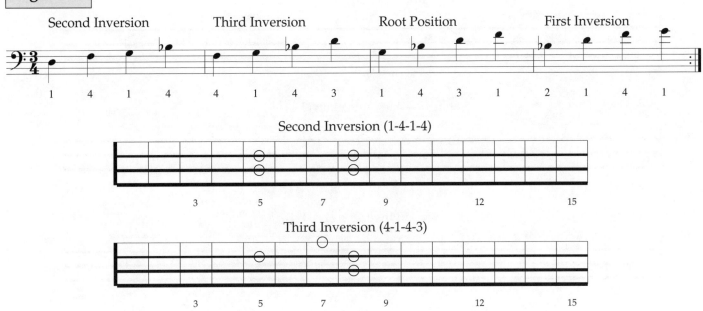

Second Inversion (1-4-1-4)

Third Inversion (4-1-4-3)

Root Position (1-4-3-1)

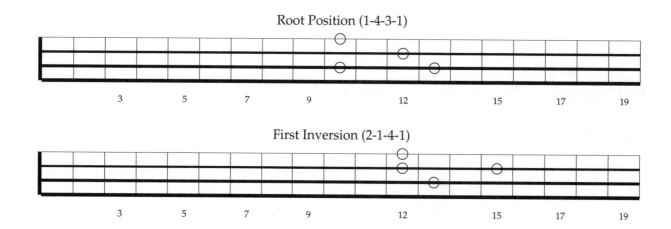

First Inversion (2-1-4-1)

D MINOR SEVENTH (Dm7)

Play the next three figures each in on area of the neck.

Figure 11

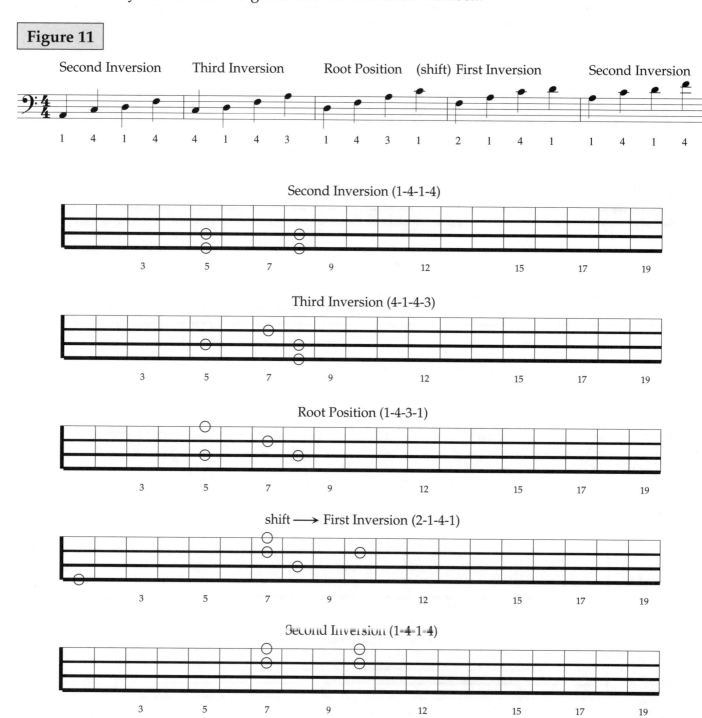

Second Inversion   Third Inversion   Root Position   (shift) First Inversion   Second Inversion

Second Inversion (1-4-1-4)

Third Inversion (4-1-4-3)

Root Position (1-4-3-1)

shift ⟶ First Inversion (2-1-4-1)

Second Inversion (1-4-1-4)

Figure 12

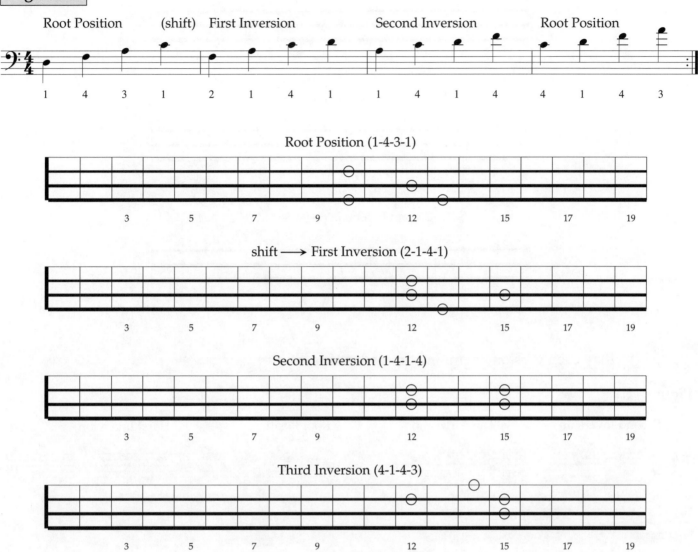

Root Position   (shift)   First Inversion   Second Inversion   Root Position

Root Position (1-4-3-1)

shift ⟶ First Inversion (2-1-4-1)

Second Inversion (1-4-1-4)

Third Inversion (4-1-4-3)

Figure 13

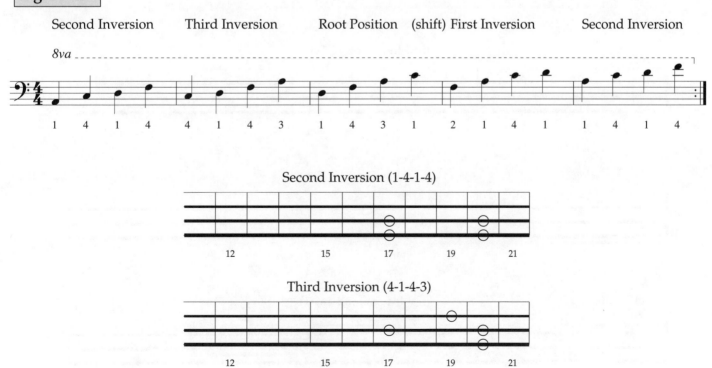

Second Inversion   Third Inversion   Root Position   (shift) First Inversion   Second Inversion

Second Inversion (1-4-1-4)

Third Inversion (4-1-4-3)

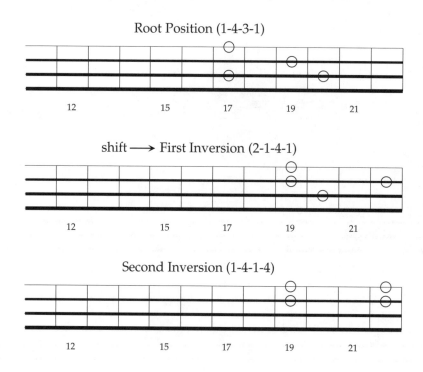

Root Position (1-4-3-1)

shift ⟶ First Inversion (2-1-4-1)

Second Inversion (1-4-1-4)

Play each version beginning on the E string.

Figure 14

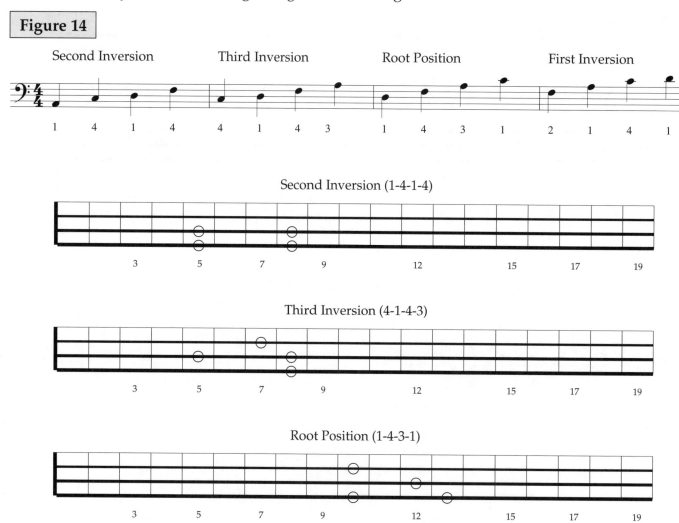

Second Inversion   Third Inversion   Root Position   First Inversion

1 4 1 4   4 1 4 3   1 4 3 1   2 1 4 1

Second Inversion (1-4-1-4)

Third Inversion (4-1-4-3)

Root Position (1-4-3-1)

First Inversion(2-1-4-1)

Play each version beginning on the A string.

Figure 15

Root Position   First Inversion   Second Inversion   Third Inversion

1   4   3   1   2   1   4   1   1   4   1   4   4   1   4   3

Root Position (1-4-3-1)

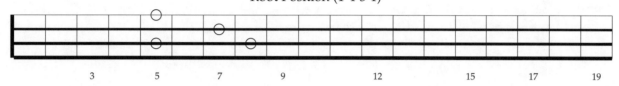

First Inversion (2-1-4-1)

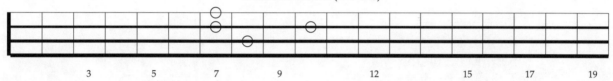

Second Inversion (1-4-1-4)

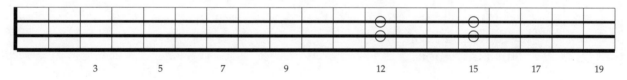

Third Inversion (4-1-4-3)

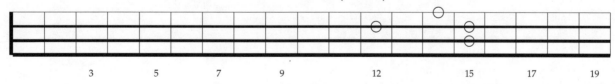

8. MINOR SEVENTH-FLAT FIVE

The last chord resulting from the harmonized major scale is the minor seventh-flat five (m7♭5). This final chord in our method will be studied exactly as the previous chord types. Follow the guidelines and instruction, and practice the arpeggios repeatedly. Although the examples revolve around fingering shapes, memorization of the spellings and sounds is crucial to a complete understanding of these arpeggios.

Practice each arpeggio using the two systems of study: first in the three general areas, played across the neck, then played up the neck, beginning from one string only. Practice the arpeggio on all root names.

The minor seventh-flat five chord is a diminished triad with a minor seventh interval added. It is equivalent to a minor seventh chord with a flatted fifth. C minor seventh-flat five is spelled: root position, C–E♭–G♭–B♭; first inversion, E♭–G♭–B♭–C; second inversion, G♭–B♭–C–E♭; and third inversion, B♭–C–E♭–G♭.

Guidelines for Minor Seventh-Flat Five

Three spellings	Notes
Root position	(1-♭3-♭5-♭7)
First inversion	(♭3-♭5-♭7-1)
Second inversion	(♭5-♭7-1-♭3)
Third inversion	(♭7-1-♭3-♭5)

One fingering shape per spelling, consistent among all root names and locations on the neck.

	Fingering
Root position	1-4-2-1
First inversion	4-2-1-3
Second inversion	2-1-3-1
Third inversion	1-3-1-4

No open strings included in fingering shape.

Arpeggiations begin with the lowest possible spelling on the fretboard.

No position shifts during the arpeggiation of a spelling—only between spellings.

Start the arpeggiation of C minor seventh-flat five with the second inverson at the second fret of the E string. Play the third inversion, make a two-fret ascending shift (first finger C on the A string), and then play root position and first inversion.

C MINOR SEVENTH-FLAT FIVE (Cm7♭5)

Figure 1

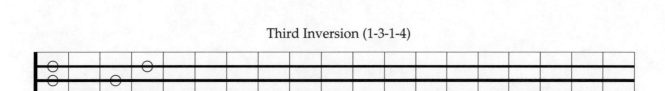

Second Inversion (2-1-3-1)

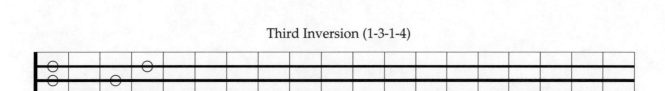

Third Inversion (1-3-1-4)

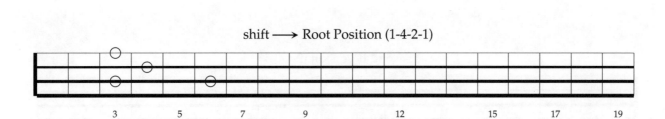

shift ⟶ Root Position (1-4-2-1)

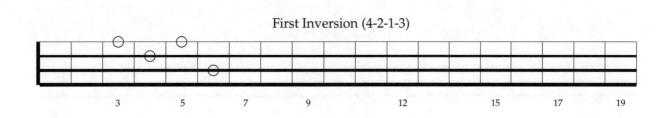

First Inversion (4-2-1-3)

75

The next area begins with the third inversion at the sixth fret of the E string. Follow this with a two-fret shift for root position, first inversion, second inversion, and a repeat of third inversion.

Figure 2

Third Inversion (shift) Root Position   First Inversion   Second Inversion   Third Inversion

Third Inversion (1-3-1-4)

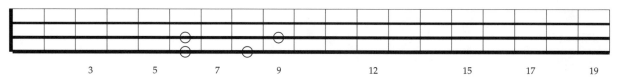

shift ⟶ Root Position (1-4-2-1)

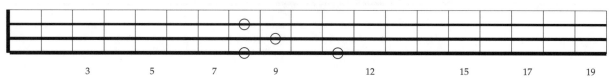

First Inversion (4-2-1-3)

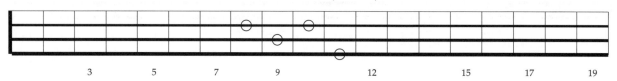

Second Inversion (2-1-3-1)

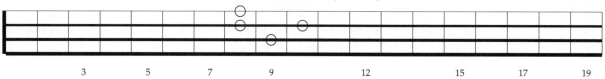

Third Inversion (1-3-1-4)

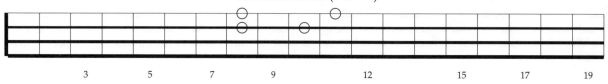

The last area duplicates the first area, up an octave, beginning at the fourteenth fret of the E string. Again start with second inversion, followed by third inversion. Then make a two-fret shift and play root position and first inversion.

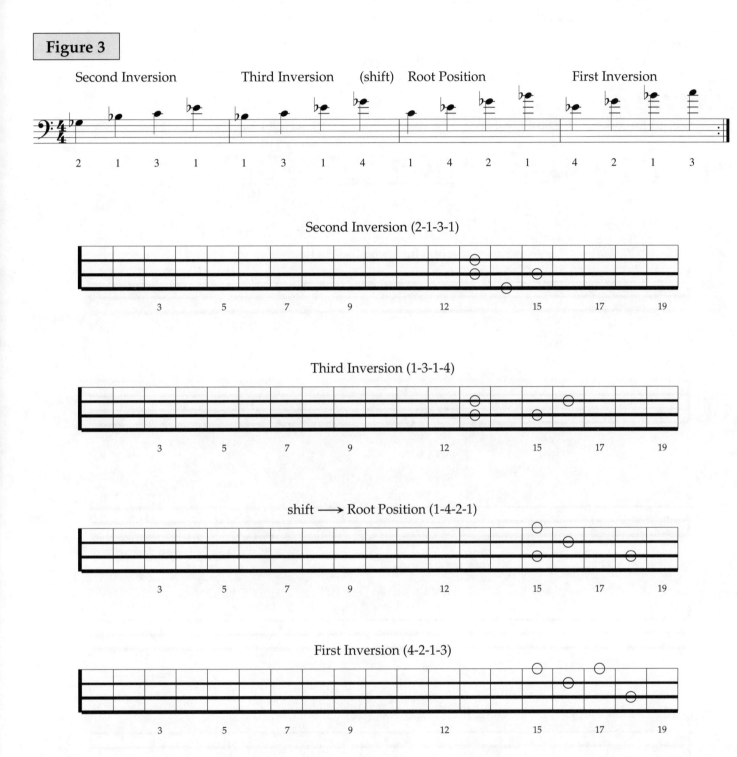

Figure 3

Review the three areas of C minor seventh-flat five and play each arpeggio over and over until spellings, shapes and locations are memorized.

Now we'll arrange each version of C minor seventh-flat five to begin on the E string. Start with second inversion at the second fret and shift to third inversion at the sixth fret. Root position and first inversion come next (first finger at the eighth fret—no shift between). Finish with a repeat of second inversion at the fourteenth fret. Remember that each shift must be smooth and connected, so the arpeggio sounds as if it was played in one area.

Play each version beginning on the E string.

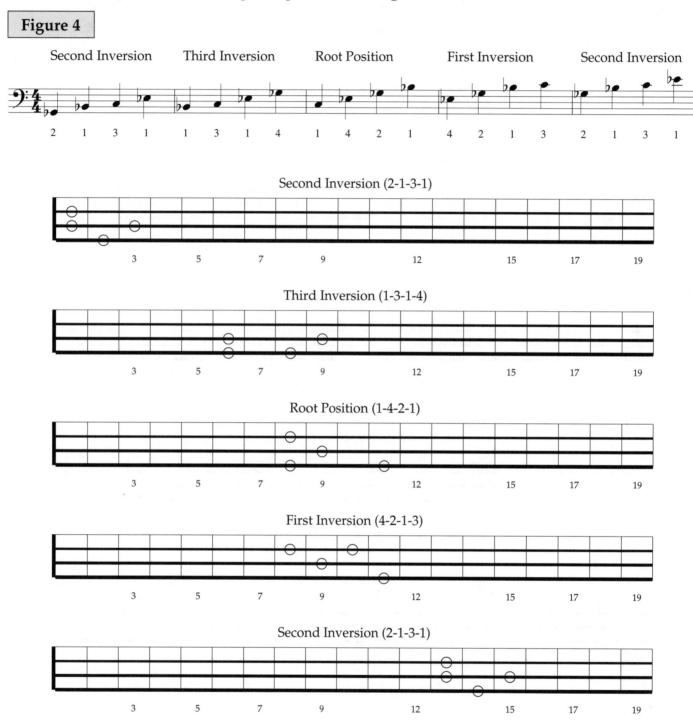

Finally, play each version starting from the A string. Third inversion begins at the first fret. Shift to the third fret to play root position. Without shifting, play the first inversion. Move to the ninth fret for second inversion, and to the thirteen fret for third inversion. Complete the arpeggio with a repeat of root position and first inversion.

Play each version beginning on the A string.

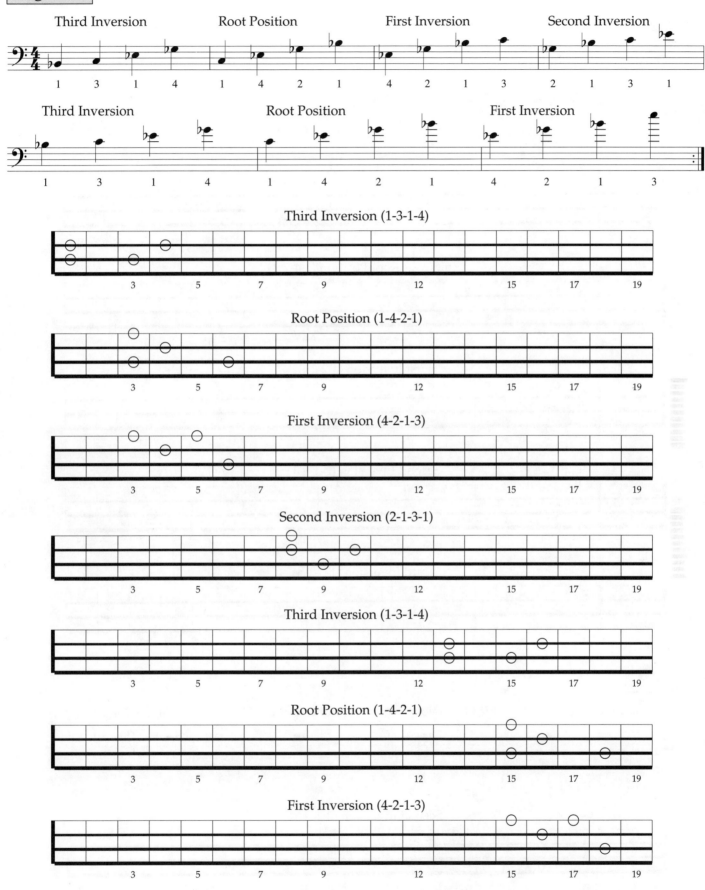

Figure 5

Review all the arpeggios for C minor seventh-flat five and play minor seventh-flat five arpeggios on all root names. G and D are provided as examples. Remember that all root names will share the same four shapes, but may start with different versions. Again as a reminder, it is very important to memorize all spellings and shapes and to sing the arpeggios as they are practiced.

G MINOR SEVENTH-FLAT FIVE (Gm7♭5)

Play the next three figures each in one area of the neck.

Figure 6

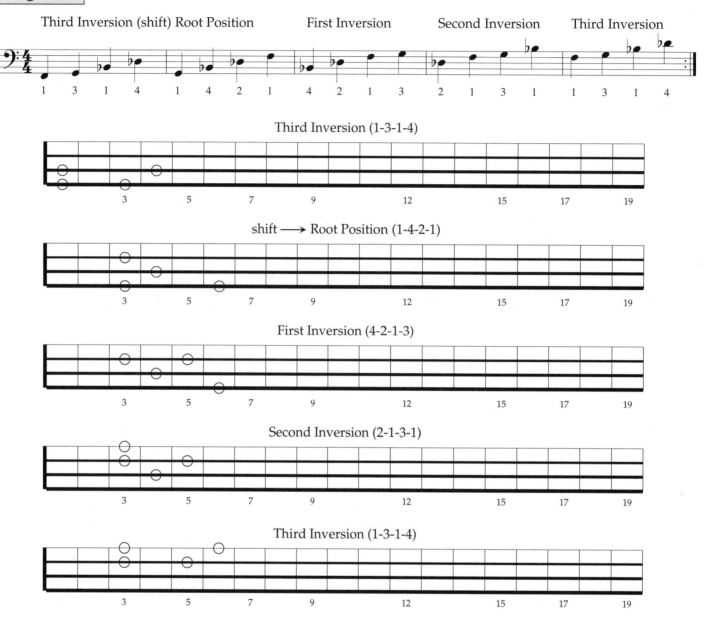

Figure 7

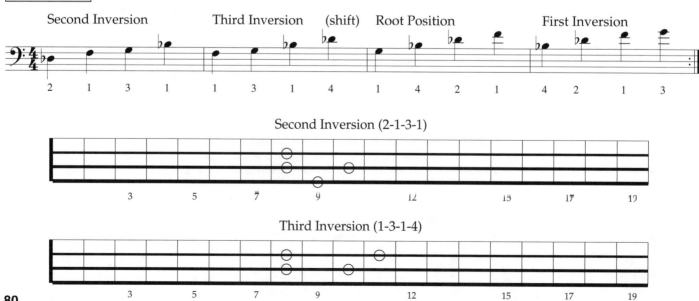

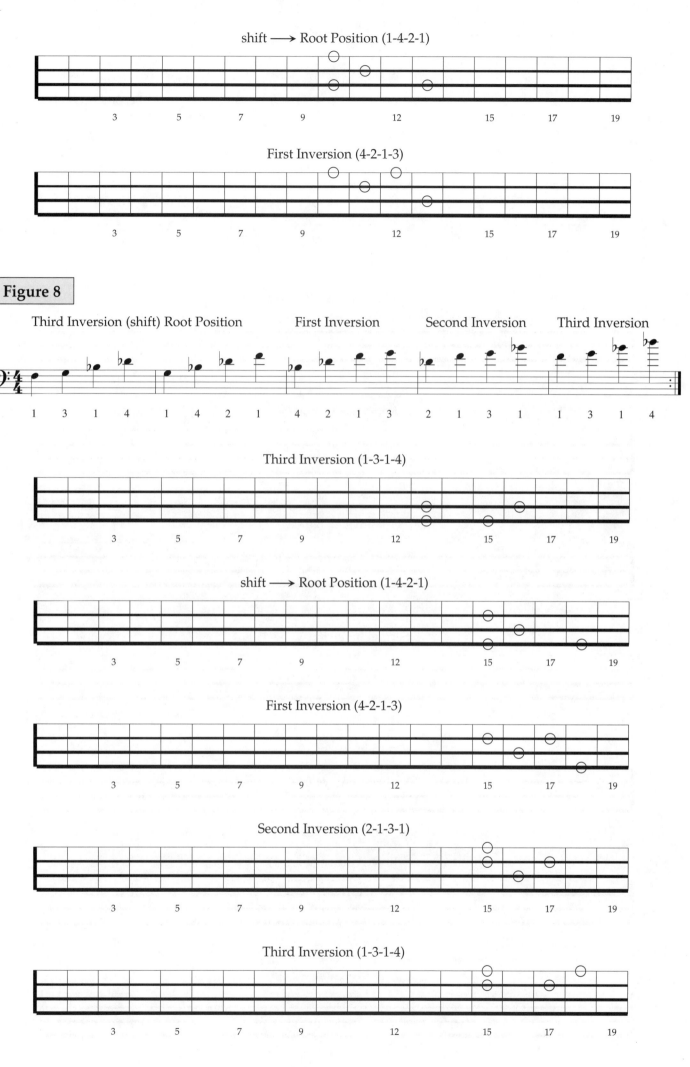

shift ⟶ Root Position (1-4-2-1)

First Inversion (4-2-1-3)

Figure 8

Third Inversion (shift) Root Position   First Inversion   Second Inversion   Third Inversion

Third Inversion (1-3-1-4)

shift ⟶ Root Position (1-4-2-1)

First Inversion (4-2-1-3)

Second Inversion (2-1-3-1)

Third Inversion (1-3-1-4)

Play each version beginning on the E string.

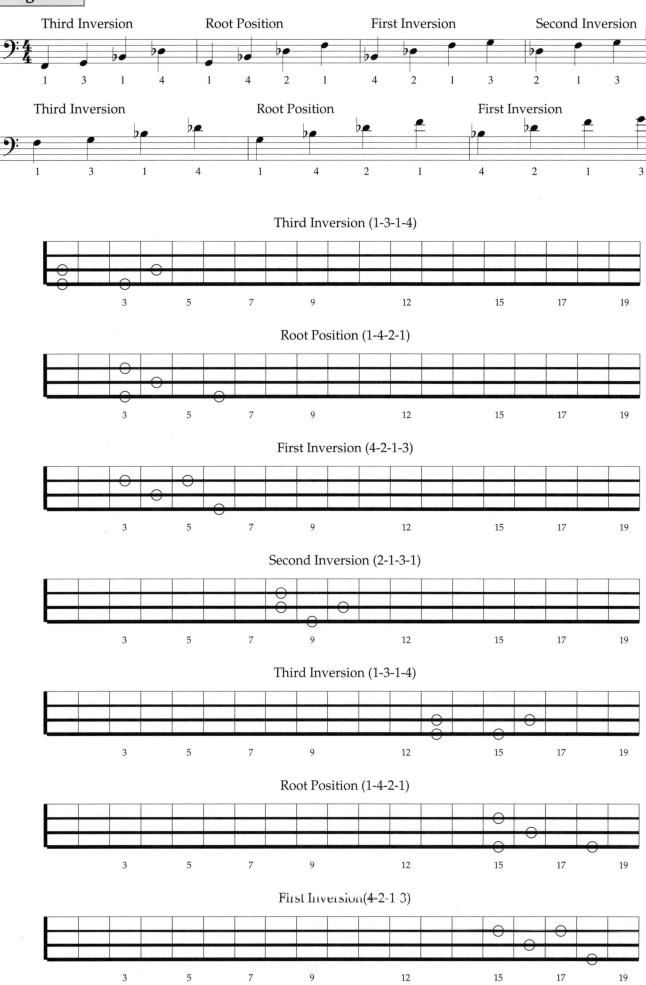

Figure 9

Third Inversion (1-3-1-4)

Root Position (1-4-2-1)

First Inversion (4-2-1-3)

Second Inversion (2-1-3-1)

Third Inversion (1-3-1-4)

Root Position (1-4-2-1)

First Inversion (4-2-1-3)

Play each version beginning on the A string.

Figure 10

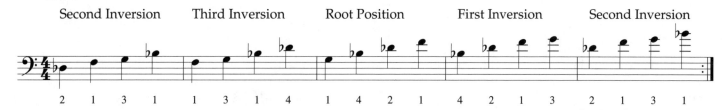

Second Inversion   Third Inversion   Root Position   First Inversion   Second Inversion

2 1 3 1   1 3 1 4   1 4 2 1   4 2 1 3   2 1 3 1

Second Inversion (2-1-3-1)

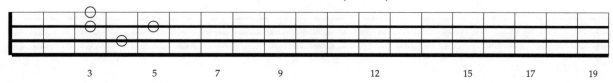

3   5   7   9   12   15   17   19

Third Inversion (1-3-1-4)

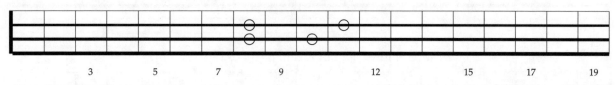

3   5   7   9   12   15   17   19

Root Position (1-4-2-1)

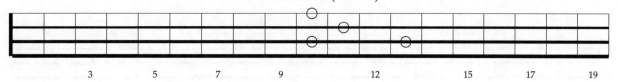

3   5   7   9   12   15   17   19

First Inversion (4-2-1-3)

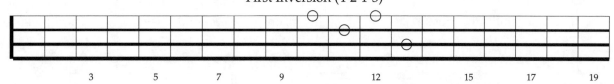

3   5   7   9   12   15   17   19

Second Inversion (2-1-3-1)

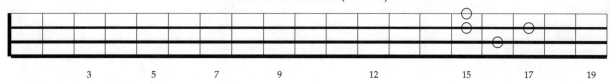

3   5   7   9   12   15   17   19

D MINOR SEVENTH-FLAT FIVE (Dm7♭5)

Play the next three figures each in one area of the neck.

Figure 11

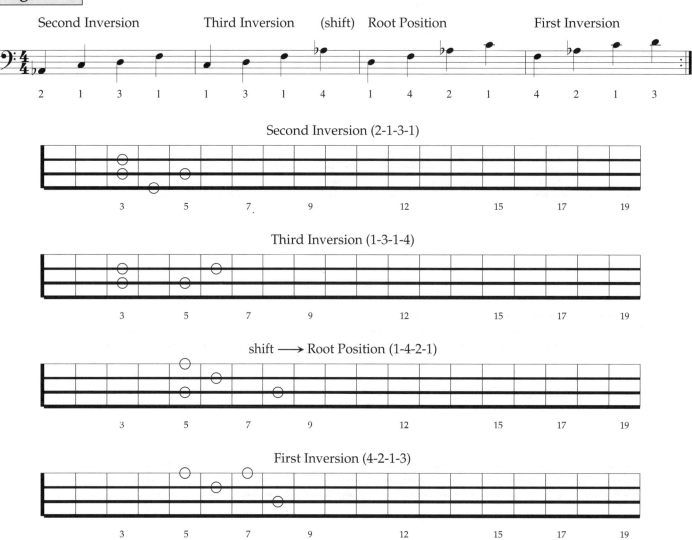

Second Inversion — Third Inversion — (shift) Root Position — First Inversion

2 1 3 1 1 3 1 4 1 4 2 1 4 2 1 3

Second Inversion (2-1-3-1)

Third Inversion (1-3-1-4)

shift ⟶ Root Position (1-4-2-1)

First Inversion (4-2-1-3)

Figure 12

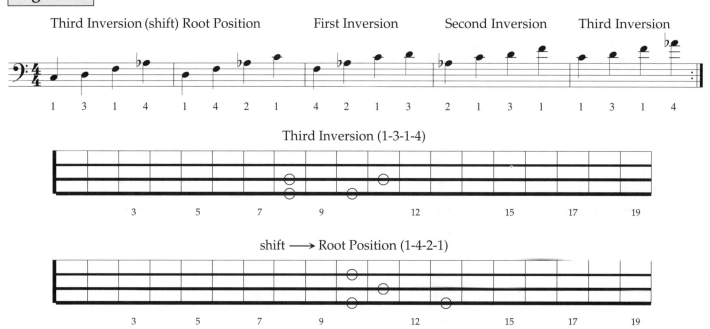

Third Inversion (shift) Root Position — First Inversion — Second Inversion — Third Inversion

1 3 1 4 1 4 2 1 4 2 1 3 2 1 3 1 1 3 1 4

Third Inversion (1-3-1-4)

shift ⟶ Root Position (1-4-2-1)

First Inversion (4-2-1-3)

Second Inversion (2-1-3-1)

Third inversion (1-3-1-4)

Figure 13

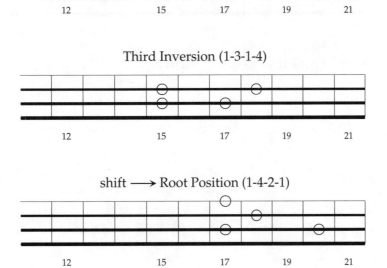

Second Inversion   Third Inversion   (shift)   Root Position   First Inversion

Second Inversion (2-1-3-1)

Third Inversion (1-3-1-4)

shift ⟶ Root Position (1-4-2-1)

First Inversion (4-2-1-3)

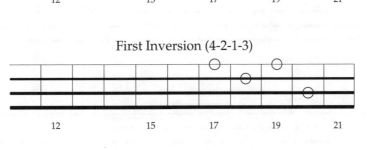

Play each version beginning on the E string.

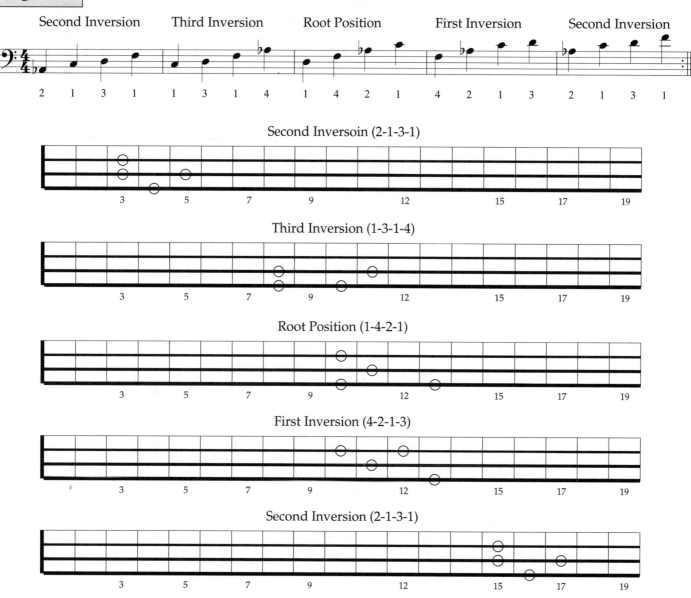

Figure 14

Play each version beginning on the A string.

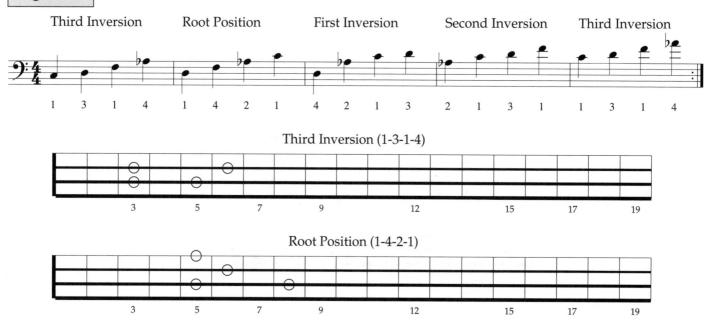

Figure 15

First Inversion (4-2-1-3)

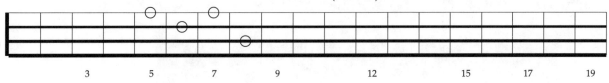

Second Inversion (2-1-3-1)

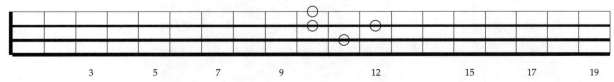

Third Inversion (1-3-1-4)

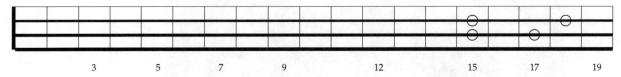

I hope this method has given you some very specific techniques for learning and applying arpeggios on the bass. In addition, there are some general lessons to be taken from this system which I would like to review.

First is the idea that an organized set of guidelines, goals, and practice habits is the best way to improve your music skills. The logical (almost mathematical) system of harmony and rhythm in music aids in this organization. Recognizing the repetitive nature of the bass neck, understanding the logic of the system, and practicing in a systematic way simplifies your learning tasks!

Second, a reminder that memorizing shapes is necessary, but not sufficient. You must also master the spellings and the sounds of this material. To be a complete musician, it is your responsibility—and in your best interest—to know as much as possible about harmony.

Finally, understand and accept the fact that reaching a high level of musicianship demands patience and hard work. Progress will seem slow and difficult at times but—above all—keep the music fun!

ABOUT THE AUTHOR

Photo by Martina Werenfeldt

David Keif teaches a variety of performance and theory classes at the Bass Institute of Technology, where he has been a core instructor since 1988. In addition to his teaching responsibilities at Musician's Institute, he maintains an active recording and performing schedule, and as a freelance bass player he has played with Kate Wolf, Rita Collidge, Etta James, and Mark Lindsay among others. He can be reached by e-mail at dknla@earthlink.net